Niue

AND THE GREAT WAR

Niue

AND THE GREAT WAR

MARGARET POINTER

OTAGO

For the people of Niue Fekai

Published by Otago University Press
Level 1, 398 Cumberland Street
Dunedin, New Zealand
university.press@otago.ac.nz
www.otago.ac.nz/press

First published 2018

ISBN 978-1-98-853123-6
A catalogue record for this book is available from the National Library of New Zealand.

Editor: Gillian Tewsley
Design/layout: Lucy Richardson
Indexer: Diane Lowther
Maps: Allan Kynaston
Printed in China through Asia Pacific Offset

Contents

Acknowledgements

Several people encouraged me to write a new edition of the Niue war story, in particular Paul Diamond, curator Māori at the Alexander Turnbull Library, who suggested it one day when I was working in the library. The original book was difficult to obtain in New Zealand and Paul suggested the story was sufficiently important to warrant a new edition.

I was convinced a new version was needed when Richard Holden of Christchurch uncovered photos from his grandparents' collection and made them available to me. Richard is the oldest surviving grandson of Joseph McMahon-Box and Annie McMahon-Box, née Head. His grandfather had moved to Niue in early 1915 to work in the New Zealand administration office and he witnessed many of the enlistment forms and photographed the departure of the Niue contingent. Richard has been very generous in allowing me to use these photos in memory of Joseph and Annie McMahon-Box.

My Niuean friends in New Zealand and on Niue have been very supportive. The families of Falaoa and Neki made contact with me after they saw my previous work on Niue contact history, published in 2015. They have been generous in sharing photos and memories and encouraging me in my work. Others have renewed earlier permissions to use family photos. Aokuso Pavihi, patron of the Niue RSA, and Moira Enetama, director of Tāoga Niue, have been a great help in answering all my email queries. Fakaaue lahi to all my Niuean friends.

I acknowledge the ongoing support of the Lawes family, both in London and in Canterbury, New Zealand. I have dined with Jonathan and Sue Lawes in London and with Frances Baylis and her family network on the Canterbury Plains – I call them all my 'missionary friends'.

Finally I wish to thank Rachel Scott and her team at Otago University Press. Rachel has been enthusiastic about the project since I first suggested it. Thank you to the anonymous reviewers in two universities who read my draft and provided useful comments and improvements and guided me in my wider reading. Thank you to Gillian Tewsley for her skilful editing of the text and Lucy Richardson for the design and layout of the book.

As ever, I value the support and encouragement of Mike and our family in bringing this work to fruition.

Fakaaue lahi, lahi tulou.

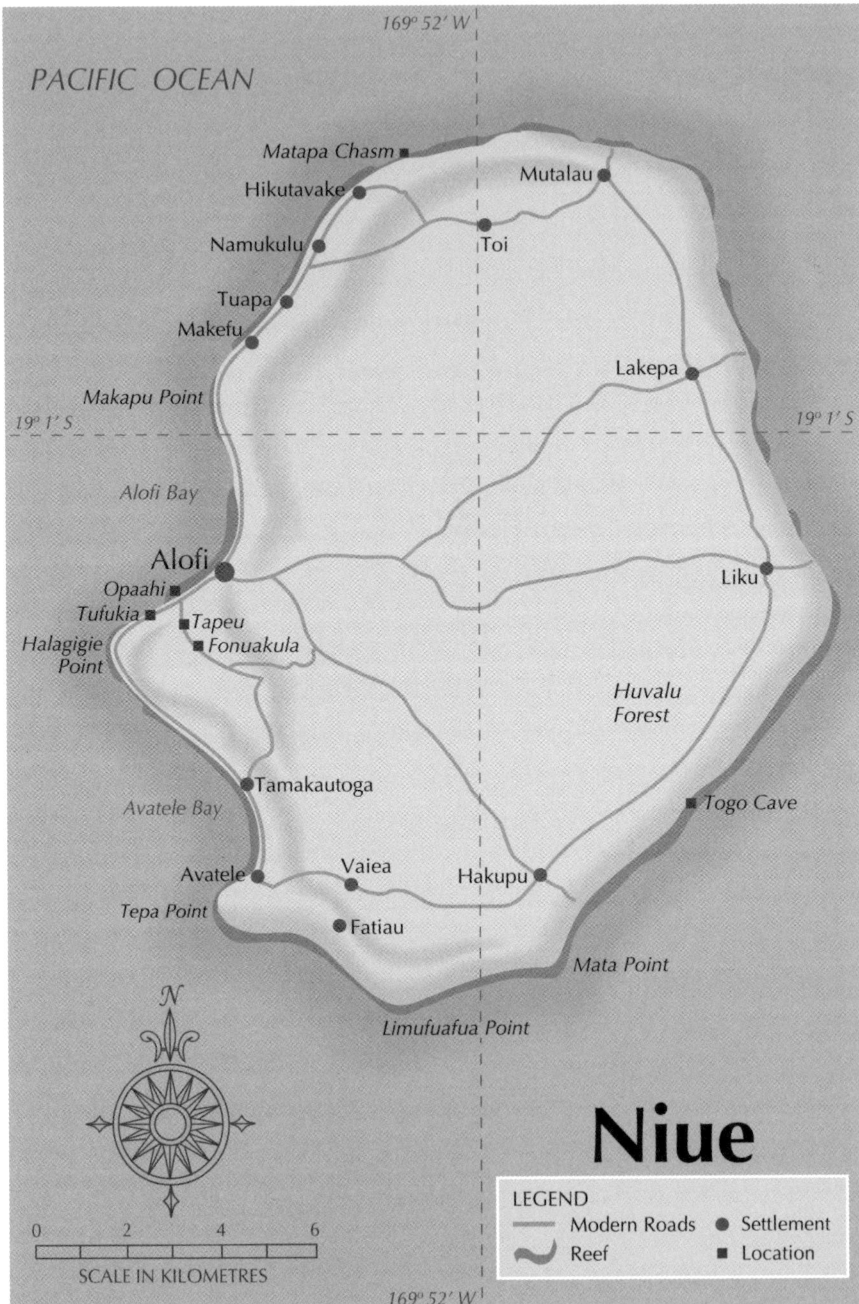

169° 52′ W
PACIFIC OCEAN
Matapa Chasm
Hikutavake
Mutalau
Namukulu
Toi
Tuapa
Makefu
Lakepa
Makapu Point
19° 1′ S
19° 1′ S
Alofi Bay
Alofi
Opaahi
Tufukia
Tapeu
Fonuakula
Halagigie Point
Liku
Huvalu Forest
Tamakautoga
Avatele Bay
Togo Cave
Avatele
Vaiea
Hakupu
Tepa Point
Fatiau
Mata Point
Limufuafua Point
N
Niue
LEGEND
Modern Roads
Reef
Settlement
Location
0
2
4
6
SCALE IN KILOMETRES
169° 52′ W

Introduction

Tuapa, 25 April 1998. It began at dawn on the green in the village of Tuapa nearly 20 years ago. Niueans had gathered to commemorate Anzac Day and acknowledge the contribution their men had made in volunteering to serve in the Great War. The sun was rising in front of us, filtering through the coconut palms that surrounded the village. The sea broke onto the reef behind us, a benign and comforting sound for the weather was good and the ocean calm. Long-tailed tropicbirds circled overhead, roosters crowed and sleepy-eyed children and dogs gradually joined the gathering. There was the smell of rich tropical foliage moistened overnight, of coconut palm branches burnt the previous evening; there was the promise of another warm day. People spoke of war in the Middle East and in Europe, of Niue helping King George V of Pelitānia, Britain, of their men sailing away and some never returning. It was impossible to reconcile the two scenes: a small, isolated tropical island lying alone, peacefully, in the vast Pacific Ocean, and the battlefields of Gallipoli and the Western Front.

As the day progressed it became clear that much of the story of Niue's involvement in the Great War had been lost. History is passed down on the island through storytelling and as people had moved off the island or died, stories had gone with them. Since that day at Tuapa I have attempted to piece the story together from official army records, war diaries, general histories of the war, newspapers of the time and the island stories I have been told. I have been privileged to have been taken into the confidence of some Niuean families who have shared what they know of their grandfathers. I wrote up what I had found, and when the book, *Tagi Tote e Loto Haaku – My Heart is Crying a Little* was launched on Niue at Anzac 2001, I thought my work was finished.[1]

The war memorial in Tuapa, on left of photo, alongside the village church. To the immediate right of the memorial is the headstone of the patuiki Togia, who made the initial offer of troops in 1914. To the extreme right is the memorial to Robert Henry Head, one of the original traders on Niue and the man who arranged for each soldier to be given a copy of the New Testament in Niuean. AUTHOR'S COLLECTION

But the story of Niue's involvement in the Great War has not left me and as the centenary of the war drew near in 2014 there was increasing interest in that story. Each time I have been asked to speak I have tried to find a new angle, I have undertaken more research. The story has been picked up by New Zealand and Australian radio and television stations, newspapers and websites.

Why has the Niue story been so embraced? There is always surprise and disbelief when people hear for the first time of the Niuean involvement. There is that disjoint we felt in Tuapa between a tropical island and the mud and cold of the Western Front. The island population was around 4000. With a small, isolated society, research becomes more focused, we can name every man, read every personnel file and then build up a story that is intensely personal. The Niue story is unique and at the same time it is universal. Small communities everywhere have their own personal and emotional connection to what

The Niue coastline as it appears today – little different from 1774 when Captain James Cook travelled along this coast. Early whalers and traders often referred to the coast as 'iron-bound' as it lacked safe harbouring or anchorage. AUTHOR'S COLLECTION

was a massive clash of empires, an incredible loss of life. This is the story of a tiny Pacific island and its connection to that war.

The centenary, which spans more than four years, has resulted in a war commemoration industry, and has had positive spinoffs. Libraries, archives and museums have prepared for this centenary and have made a huge quantity of material available in a format that can be easily accessed. Twenty years ago I read individual newspapers in search of stories relating to the Niueans; now powerful search engines can check for stories in seconds. Army personnel files in New Zealand have been digitised in preparation for the centenary and historians have worked hard to tell thousands of stories that personalise the war. Many image collections have been digitised and placed online and, most importantly, more images of Niueans have been uncovered.

Internationally there has been an increasing interest and focus on colonial involvement and how the war impacted on far-flung countries. As one writer put it, what have in the past been considered 'sideshows in the grand

European narrative of the war' were, in fact, 'momentous events with enduring consequences for the local communities'.[2] Alongside this more comprehensive consideration of the global impact of the war is an emphasis on the tragedy of war – what the poet Wilfred Owen called 'the pity of war'.[3] The Niue story has slotted into both these considerations and writers have seized on it to demonstrate the involvement of remote communities and the impact and tragedy of the war for those communities.[4]

As the story of the Niuean involvement began to take shape for me, I realised this was, more than anything else, a very sad story, a story of ordinary men in extraordinary circumstances; frightened, bewildered, uncomprehending, homesick, ill. The high rate of hospitalisation – over 80 per cent by the time the Niueans were stationed in France – was acknowledged in the decision to withdraw the group from the Western Front, but the medical authorities glossed over the impact of European diseases on people from isolated communities. Illness – particularly in the form of pneumonia, pleurisy and tuberculosis – was attributed to 'lack of stamina' or 'Niue Island constitution'.[5] These 'reasons' for discharge perhaps added to the stigma of their not being able to 'cope' in war, which may account for a reluctance on the part of the army authorities to examine the Niuean contribution to the New Zealand war effort until very recent times. In 2015 the New Zealand Defence Force added the names of three more Niueans, Alotau, Mitipauni and Muimatagi, to the Roll of Honour, acknowledging that although these men had died of pneumonia after discharge from the army, their deaths were directly attributable to their war service. There are other men who may merit similar reconsideration.

Lack of immunity to disease was a major cause of deaths during the war, and it was not limited to Niueans – Cook Islanders, Tahitians, Kanak of New Caledonia and many other populations were affected. Concentrations of personnel in transport ships, army camps, in the trenches and even in the military hospitals contributed hugely to the death toll. In addition, army authorities were very reluctant to recognise shell shock (now a recognised condition, post-traumatic stress disorder). The Niuean men suffered their share of these problems – some, no doubt, long after they arrived back on Niue.

Private Pimeleko of Mutalau. Pimeleko sailed with the main body from Auckland to Egypt and then to France. He returned from Hornchurch with the second group of Niueans on the Arawa *in July 1916.* COURTESY OF MRS FASA TONGAKILO, MUTALAU, NIUE

A revised edition of the original work seemed timely, not only because of a general shift in emphasis from military to social and personal history, or because of the great increase in archival material available to tell a fuller story, but also because I realised that the Niue story needs to be placed in a wider context – both a Pacific context and an imperial context. In this edition I have considered the entire Pacific as a region of imperial rivalry and then as a theatre of imperial war. The Niue contribution to the war effort must be seen as part of a wider contribution from throughout the Pacific – from Rarotonga, Mangaia, Aitutaki, Atiu, Pukapuka, Rakahanga, Mauke, Manihiki, Penrhyn, Mitiaro, all islands in the Cook group; from Suva, Nadi, Bau, Levuka in Fiji; from New Caledonia and French Polynesia; from Tonga; from Samoa; from the Gilbert and Ellice Islands.

Within the British imperial context, the position of indigenous troops from throughout the empire must be considered. The British government was very happy to accept white colonials into the British Expeditionary Force, but many non-white colonials also volunteered. This did not sit comfortably with prevailing eurocentric views: there was a belief that using 'black and coloured' troops would 'undermine the dignity of the white man'[6] – whether such troops were ranged alongside or against white troops. However, the British army soon discovered that to mount a war on several fronts and over so many parts of the globe at the same time required a huge support structure, and the offer of troops from many British colonies and territories provided the labour for the war effort. From India and Ceylon, Kenya and Uganda, Swaziland and Bechuanaland, from South Africa, from Egypt and China, from the West Indies and Mauritius and from the scattered islands of the Pacific came men by the hundreds of thousands to support the war machine. They carried supplies, loaded and unloaded vessels, stood guard, manned ammunition dumps, dug trenches and built duckboards, served food and cleaned latrines. The recognition that these troops were a vital part of the war effort has been slow in coming, but the centenary has resulted in greater acknowledgement of them.

On Niue it was apparent that there were two omissions from the story that were the cause of deep hurt for some families. The first was the absence of any information about the men who volunteered for service with the Niue contingent and who sailed to New Zealand for training in October 1915 but who, because of illness, were unable to continue on to Egypt: their names do not appear on the New Zealand army's nominal rolls, as these recorded the names of men leaving New Zealand after training had been completed. Their names are included on some memorials on the island, but omitted from others.[7] The name of one man, Vilipate, who died during training in Auckland, was not included on the marble tablet prepared for the war memorial unveiled on the island in 1920 – yet the purpose of this tablet was to record the names of the men who had died while in service.

The second omission was of the men from Niue who served, not in the Niue contingent, but in other parts of the New Zealand Expeditionary Force (NZEF). These were generally men who had been working in New Zealand and who enlisted there. The increase in available archival material has enabled me to rectify both these omissions, to some extent.

Central to the purpose of this revised edition is the question of whether knowledge of Niuean history can give pride and strength to those still on Niue, and help those who have left reconnect to their island.[8] There is anecdotal evidence that this is possible. Perhaps the most telling proof that knowledge of their history can give people a sense of belonging and serve to reconnect them to their homeland came in October 2015 when the Niue government held a commemoration for the 100th anniversary of the men leaving for war.[9]

As always when I reflect on researching and writing on the subject of Niue's involvement in the Great War, I remember the words of my old friend Sifa.[10] Daughter of Private Tio of Alofi, she was one of the last surviving children of a serviceman and she embraced my first work. In church at Avatele on Anzac Day 2001, Sifa stood up to speak. 'I like this book,' she said, waving a copy. 'I really like this book. And do you know why I like this book? Because it's got my name in it.' That is the essence of this work. It is about Niue and Niueans. They take centre stage in their own story. If they find it useful then it has been worth writing.

THE JOURNEY TO WAR AND HOME

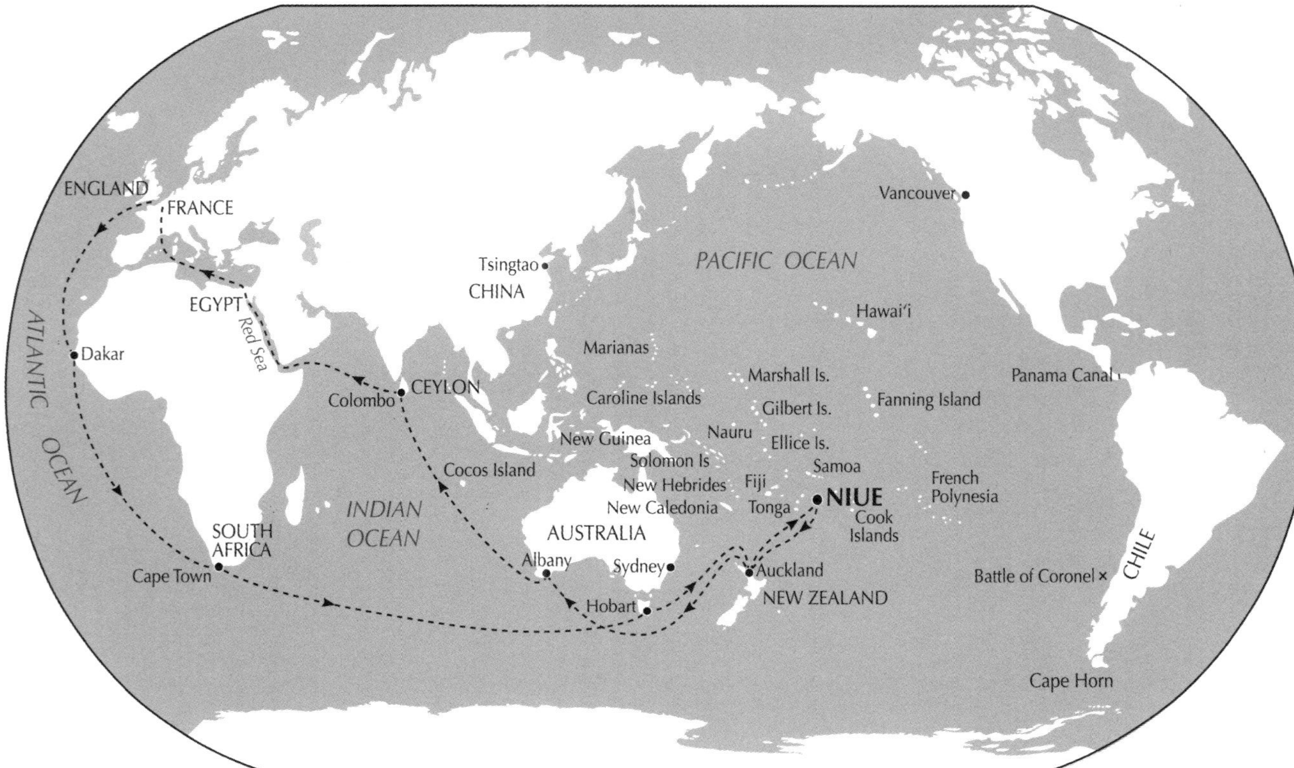

CHAPTER 1

Background to war: A Pacific perspective

The Pacific Ocean is, in the words of one writer, 'so vast that its size can be calibrated only in extremes and superlatives. An area of nearly 180 million square kilometres; a breadth that at its greatest span approaches 20,000 kilometres; an expanse that appears largely empty yet is strewn with more than 25,000 islands.'[1] It is the vastness of the Pacific that is so difficult to comprehend – the geographical fragmentation of tiny islands, the great distances between them and the multiplicity and richness of societies that have developed in isolation from other parts of the world.

The islands are of two main types: the high volcanic islands with their green peaks clad in tropical forest; and the atolls, fragments of coral reef that originally circled an ancient volcano and now form a low-lying perimeter around an inner lagoon. What they lack in lush vegetation the atolls make up for in the intense blues of the lagoon and of the waves breaking on the coral reef. Then there is the occasional island created by tectonic uplift so that the drained lagoon now rests high above sea level with the old coral reef still circling it, hardened and eroded into an unforgiving surface.

Voyagers from the western side of the Pacific traversed the ocean in double-hulled canoes loaded with foodstuffs such as coconut, banana, taro, arrowroot and yams.[2] Travelling in both directions and using prodigious navigational skills based on memorised star charts and a knowledge of seasonal changes of ocean and wind currents, these people gradually settled the remote islands, and each island settlement developed its own unique society with its particular language and culture. While some islands or island groups supported populations in the tens of thousands, others could only support very small numbers, in the hundreds or low thousands.

Europeans were late to discover this vast section of the globe. The earliest explorers were the Spanish and the Portuguese in the fifteenth and sixteenth centuries, followed by the Dutch, French and English in the seventeenth and eighteenth centuries. After the explorers came the whalers, traders and missionaries: whalers came for the precious oil to light the lamps back home; traders came for sandalwood, bêche-de-mer and pearlshell; companies were set up to process sugarcane and copra or to harvest guano for fertiliser; the blackbirders came for labour, often forced, to take to the pineapple and sugar plantations of Queensland and Fiji; and missionaries came in search of men's souls. By the end of the nineteenth century all Pacific islands were, to a greater or lesser extent, under European control.

Reverend Frank and Mrs Sarah Lawes in the mission house garden in Alofi in the 1880s. The Lawes family served with the London Missionary Society on Niue from 1868 until 1910 when they retired to London. They were instrumental in binding the Niuean people to the concept of the British Empire and the importance of Queen Victoria.
COURTESY OF THE LAWES FAMILY, LONDON

As the European powers established spheres of influence in the Pacific, imperial rivalry increased in the region. There was competition for direct control of particular island territories as protectorates or colonies. By the mid-nineteenth century Britain dominated the region, for it had already established colonies in Australia and New Zealand and regarded the Pacific Ocean as an important sphere of influence. Fiji, with its central location in the vast ocean, became a crown colony in 1874. The British also established protectorate status over the Gilbert and Ellice Islands, the Solomon Islands, southeastern New Guinea, the Cook Islands and Niue. Tonga, the only Pacific island to remain independent, accepted the status of protected state in a treaty of friendship with Britain in 1900. France established a protectorate and then a colony in New Caledonia, Wallis and Futuna and the island groups centred on Tahiti and known collectively as French Polynesia. France and Britain both claimed the New Hebrides and, in 1906, finally settled on joint sovereignty. By the late nineteenth century two new powers were exerting influence in the Pacific region: Germany claimed the northeastern portion of New Guinea and then Nauru as colonies in the 1880s, and then bought the Marshall Islands, the Caroline Islands and the Marianas from a weakened Spanish government; and the United States annexed the Hawaiian Islands in 1898. Britain, Germany and the United States attempted to jointly administer the Samoa group but, when this failed, the islands were divided in 1899 between Germany and the United States.

The widely scattered islands of the Pacific were now under European control but there was still the huge expanse of ocean separating territories from each other and from the metropoles. The solution to this was to create strong shipping links. Here again Britain dominated as the development of steam and steel resulted in bigger and faster vessels, and the Royal Navy expanded to protect those sea links. A Royal Navy squadron based in Sydney from the mid-nineteenth century regularly patrolled the British Pacific territories until 1911 when the Royal Australian Navy was established and assumed some of these duties. Germany undertook a massive naval building programme in the lead-up to the Great War, and as Pacific territories were acquired, the German

The German East Asia Squadron in Apia Harbour before the outbreak of war. From left are the warships Emden, Leipzig, Scharnhorst, Condor *and* Cormoran. *Western Samoa was a German territory and an important refuelling base for the German vessels.*
SIR GEORGE GREY SPECIAL COLLECTIONS, AUCKLAND LIBRARIES, NEW ZEALAND, AWNS-19141022-36-2 (A.J. TATTERSALL)

East Asia Squadron was based in the German concessionary port of Tsingtao on the coast of China to protect German interests in the Pacific.

It was not only shipping that connected empires, but the development of the telegraph cable. The British network of submarine and overland cables created what one historian has called 'the imperial information highway'.[3] Two cable routes of particular importance to the Pacific were the one that crossed the Indian Ocean from South Africa to Australia; and the cable that traversed the Pacific Ocean from Vancouver to Fiji, and on to New Zealand and Australia.

Tiny Niue, lying alone in the Pacific, benefited from neither good shipping links nor telegraph communications. The island is an old uplifted coral atoll with terraces at 30 and 60 metres above sea level; there are no protective harbours and, indeed, no anchoring, as the land drops steeply from the fringing reef into the deep ocean. It was settled approximately 1000 years ago by people from Tonga to the west and Samoa to the north; they developed their own distinctive language and culture on Niue, isolated as they were from other groups. The earliest name for their home was Nukutūtaha, the island that stands alone.

Niue first appeared on European maps after the second voyage of Captain James Cook. He landed on the island briefly in 1774 but received what he considered a very unfriendly reception; when he sailed away he marked it 'Savage Island' on his Pacific chart. By the mid-nineteenth century Niue had come within the unofficial orbit of Britain. The arrival of missionaries from the London Missionary Society (LMS) and their successful establishment on the island, along with two or three English traders, meant that Niueans were taught about the benefits of the British Empire and learnt to love Queen Victoria. The Island Council, consisting of elders representing all the villages and advised by the English missionary Reverend Frank Lawes, a resident on the island for over 40 years, made several requests to become part of the great British Empire: 'We desire to pray your Majesty and your Majesty's kingdom if it be your pleasure, to stretch out towards us your mighty hand, that Niue may hide herself in it and be safe. We are afraid lest some other powerful nation should come and trouble us ...'[4]

The island became a formal protectorate early in 1900 and was annexed a few months later. But by this time Britain, which was deeply committed to the war in South Africa (the Boer War), had realised that colonies were financially and economically draining; within a year, it handed the administration of Niue – and the Cook Islands – to New Zealand, which had long lobbied the British government for a role in the Pacific. The motives for this were mixed, but geographical proximity meant New Zealand was interested in the region for commercial and strategic reasons and the premier of the time, Richard

A scene in Alofi in 1900. The influence of the LMS is clear: women in full-length missionary dresses, and neat white houses and walls. Cleanliness and orderliness were essential features of mission rule. RANFURLY COLLECTION, ALEXANDER TURNBULL LIBRARY, WELLINGTON, NEW ZEALAND, PA1-Q-633_036

Seddon, saw a Pacific empire as a counterbalance to the influence of the federation recently formed by the amalgamation of Australian colonies.[5]

Although Niue became a New Zealand territory, this did not mean attention turned away from Britain: the LMS enjoyed a monopoly on the island and, when the Lawes returned to London in 1910, their replacement came from England; the LMS headquarters were in London; funds were raised on the island and sent to London for worldwide missionary activities; congregations in Britain collected money and goods to send to the mission on Niue; schools on the island were run almost exclusively by the church and placed a strong emphasis on learning about Britain and the Empire; New Zealand officials and traders on the island were nearly all born in Britain or were of British parentage.

Whatever its political status, Niue remained extremely isolated. Seddon from New Zealand promised to provide a regular steamship service between the island and Auckland, but by 1914 this had not eventuated. Shipping was sporadic and, during the cyclone season from November to March, virtually non-existent. Nor was there any radio link with the outside world; news arrived when a vessel arrived, and it could be months out of date.

Life on the island was very much centred on the village, the church and the bush, where each family grew crops for their own needs and to support their village church. There were small trading stores dotted around the island, but supplies were often limited or even scarce, and Islanders depended largely on locally grown crops. Cyclones and drought meant life was often difficult. With no protected lagoon, fishermen had to go out into the Pacific in their small vaka, canoes, and conditions often made this dangerous or impossible. Some of the young men travelled away from the island as contract labourers on German copra plantations in Samoa, British plantations in Tonga or French ones in Tahiti. Some went to remote guano islands near the equator to work for British companies; others crewed on vessels in the Pacific. At the end of their contract most were returned to the island. Other Niueans had never left the island. Most people spoke only Vagahau Niue, and the Pālagi or European population on the island numbered barely 30 of a total population of around 4000.

When competition among the imperial powers descended into war in 1914, the Pacific was drawn into the conflict along with the rest of the world. There was a rapid seizure of German territories in the Pacific: New Zealand captured German Samoa and Australia seized German New Guinea, the Bismarck Archipelago and Nauru, while in the north Pacific, Japan – a British ally in this conflict – took the Caroline and Marshall Islands and the Marianas.

The rising generation. Boys sitting on the wall of the mission house in Alofi watching the first New Zealand parliamentary visit to Niue in 1903. By 1915 these boys were old enough to join the Niue contingent to World War I.

MUSEUM OF NEW ZEALAND TE PAPA TONGAREWA, HENRY WINKELMANN LS 005307

From its base at Tsingtao, the German East Asia Squadron under the command of the vice-admiral Count Maximilian von Spee spread out across the Pacific. Outnumbered and outgunned by Allied navies in the region and conscious of the fact that he was cut off from home ports in Germany, von Spee set out to do as much damage as possible to those two lifelines of empire: shipping routes and communication cables. One cruiser was deployed to the Indian Ocean to attack Allied merchant and naval vessels. It met with considerable success until, in November 1914, it attacked the Cocos Islands, an important relay station on the Indian Ocean cable route. A mayday message from the station alerted the Australian navy, which was in the area accompanying troop transport vessels from New Zealand and Australia. HMAS *Sydney* broke away from the convoy and destroyed the German vessel. The other five vessels in the German squadron were in the Pacific. A raiding party landed on Fanning Island in the northern Line Islands in September 1914: they destroyed the telegraph instruments and cut the submarine cable.

Meanwhile New Zealand had landed a force in Samoa in late August 1914. They met with no resistance from the German authorities and their capture of the wireless station in Apia – a vital part of the communications network used by German shipping in the Pacific – reduced von Spee's effectiveness. Realising that Allied activity in the Pacific had increased greatly, he decided to move his fleet around Cape Horn into the Atlantic and northwards in an attempt to reach Germany. As he sailed across the Pacific he bombed the main French port of Pape'ete, in Tahiti, in late September and then, off the coast of Chile, von Spee attacked and sank two British cruisers in November 1914: all 1570 lives were lost on the British vessels while the Germans recorded three men wounded. A month later, however, when the squadron rounded Cape Horn and headed into the Atlantic it was met by a British force and annihilated, with the loss of over 2000 German lives.[6] The German East Asia Squadron was at an end.

These early naval battles made it easier subsequently for Britain and France to source supplies and men from their respective colonial territories in the Pacific, and in the course of four years people from throughout the Pacific

Battle at Cocos Island in November 1914: a full-page spread that appeared in the Auckland Weekly News. *The caption reads, 'The last raid of the* Emden: *Photographs taken at Cocos Island during the wrecking of the cable station and the destruction of the German cruiser on November 9'. The photo top left shows the HMAS* Sydney *off Cocos Island.* SIR GEORGE GREY SPECIAL COLLECTIONS, AUCKLAND LIBRARIES, NEW ZEALAND, AWNS-19150107-39-1

'Germany's loss, Britain's gain: Hoisting the Union Jack at the courthouse, Apia, on the morning of 30 August'. Following a request from the British government to seize the German territory, the Samoa Advance Party of the NZEF arrived in Apia on 29 August. A New Zealand-run British military occupation of German Samoa was proclaimed the next day. It was the second territory seized from Germany since war had been declared.
SIR GEORGE GREY SPECIAL COLLECTIONS, AUCKLAND LIBRARIES, NEW ZEALAND, AWNS-19140917-43-2 (A.J. TATTERSALL)

went to serve in Europe and the Middle East. Australia and New Zealand were vitally important to the British war effort. Both countries – former British colonies and now self-governing dominions – supplied large expeditionary forces that were constantly reinforced with more recruits.[7] These forces served as part of the British Expeditionary Force, but as the war progressed the dominions increasingly asserted their independence and became more directly involved in military and political decision-making: from 1917 their leaders were included in an imperial war cabinet in London.

Men came from elsewhere in the Pacific, too. The British crown colony of Fiji supplied contingents of Europeans and, later, an indigenous Fijian labour corps directly to Britain. Contingents from the Cook Islands and Niue joined the New Zealand Expeditionary Force. Individual men came to New Zealand from Samoa, Tonga, Fiji and the Gilbert and Ellice Islands to enlist in the NZEF. Towards the end of the war an ethnically mixed contingent from Fiji and a small group of native police from the Gilbert and Ellice Islands were accepted for training in New Zealand at the request of the British authorities; they were still in training when the Armistice was signed in November 1918.[8]

France also received assistance from its Pacific territories – New Caledonia and French Polynesia. When news of war reached these areas there was concern at the presence of the German navy in the Pacific, and this increased greatly with the bombardment of Pape`ete. Men from both French territories were keen to enlist and from early 1916 'native subjects' also became eligible to volunteer.[9] A Bataillon mixte du Pacifique was created and dispatched to the Western Front and reinforcements were sent throughout the war; the Tahitian contingents passed through New Zealand en route to join the New Caledonian contingents in Sydney.[10]

Right from the outbreak of war the Pacific was therefore involved. German territories were seized and placed under military occupation for the duration of the war. The German East Asia fleet stalked the ocean and caused considerable anxiety, damage and loss of life until it was defeated by the British in the southern Atlantic. And from the Pacific came men and supplies to assist the war effort in the Middle East and Europe: they came from Australia and New Zealand, from Fiji, New Caledonia and Tahiti and from tiny atolls and islands scattered throughout the South Pacific – including the small island of Niue.

DETAIL: *Soldiers of the Maori Contingent on Wellington wharf, 14 February 1915.*
ALEXANDER TURNBULL LIBRARY, WELLINGTON, NEW ZEALAND, 1/2-011079-F

CHAPTER 2

Preparation for war

News of the outbreak of war in August 1914 took some time to reach Niue. One vessel, the barque *Ysabel*, had called at the island in late August but it had left Auckland before the declaration of war so Captain Ross, the master and owner of the vessel, had no news of it. He was very surprised, when he reached the Hauraki Gulf on his return to Auckland, to have searchlights trained on him and his vessel delayed pending an inspection because of new Defence Department regulations. When he berthed Ross expressed concern for the inhabitants of Niue and the Tonga group, who still knew nothing about the hostilities.[1]

Because it was winter in the Pacific and not the cyclone season, the shipping to Niue was more frequent and, as the *Ysabel* was berthing in Auckland, the ketch *Kereru* was departing for Niue. After a fast run north it arrived on 12 September with supplies, mail and the news that Europe was at war. Captain Anderson reported that five German cruisers had been sighted among the islands and that German Samoa had surrendered to a New Zealand force at the end of the previous month. On his return to Auckland, Anderson reported that 'the news of the outbreak of war caused the greatest excitement on the island'.[2] Reverend James Cullen, the newly arrived resident missionary on the island, wrote:

> The last vessel brought us the terrible news of war, though our news is very meagre. How awful it is and how impossible for us to realise all that it must be for those at home. We are racked with anxiety as to what may happen to our dear ones, but our utter helplessness throws us more entirely upon God. Even in this distant island we are greatly affected.[3]

During the five days that the *Kereru* lay in Alofi Bay, funds were collected on the island to send back to New Zealand for the war effort: £164 14s 5d was presented to Captain Anderson for the Empire Defence Fund, including £131 15s 2d donated by Niueans and £32 19s 3d by the European residents.[4]

The Island Council also met with resident commissioner Henry Cornwall and drew up an offer of troops. The idea for this very likely came from the Pālagi residents but it was taken up enthusiastically by the council, and they asked Cornwall to report to his government that 'the natives are eager to render further assistance and offer the services of 200 able-bodied young natives for service anywhere they may be required'.[5] The 12 members of the council wrote and signed a letter, expressed in a similar vein to nineteenth-century requests for British protection. The letter was destined to be widely reported:

> To King George V, all those in authority, and the brave men who fight: I am the island of Niue, a small child that stands up to help the Kingdom of King George V. There are two portions we are offering: (1) money; (2) men.[6]

Cornwall later acknowledged that one Niuean elder in particular had been pivotal in gaining island support. Uea, a respected pastor, 'was the principal means of the contribution to the War Fund being made and the offer of 200 men and he has been the mainstay throughout in the matter. Uea has been a pastor for over 20 years and would, I think, be acceptable to the men as their chaplain.'[7]

The offer, read out by the prime minister in the New Zealand parliament and reported in the New Zealand press, was cabled to London, and by December 1914 it was being reported as 'Loyal offer from a Savage Island', 'Niue Island natives and the war' and 'a quaint offer … by the aborigines of Niue, or Savage Island'.[8] Cornwall's covering letter to his government in Wellington did caution, however, that 'the offer is made in the best possible spirit, but it is only fair to say that the natives could not possibly provide or pay for the equipment, and, further, they do not understand any language but their own'.[9] The response on Niue to the news of war was spontaneous and heartfelt: as in other communities throughout the empire, they enthusiastically

16/1176 Sergeant Major Uea, chaplain in the Niue contingent. Uea, a respected pastor on Niue, was instrumental in gaining island support for a contingent and went with the group as their chaplain. He is photographed on arrival in Auckland with his son Makanetiaki, a student at St Stephen's College in Auckland.

COURTESY OF MARION AND KAREN MCQUOID, AUCKLAND

embraced the ideals of duty and loyalty to the King.[10] The *Kereru* sailed from Niue with the money and the offer of men, and the island hunkered down for another cyclone season. Nothing further would be heard of the war in general, or the offer from Niue in particular, for several months.

The traders saw the immediate impact of war in the increase in prices of many imported goods. Foreseeing a disruption in trade they immediately dropped the price they were prepared to pay for local export crops and, in some cases, stopped buying altogether. Niue was going to have to rely on the local food crops such as taro, yam, banana and coconut. This was not difficult if weather conditions were favourable, but a strong cyclone in January 1915 and a drought in the following months meant supplies were scarce. The situation for Niueans was not as dire as in Tonga, though; there, high prices over a long period for cash crops, especially copra, had led to a marked decline in the production of local food crops and a high dependence on flour, biscuits and canned meat from Auckland.[11]

In Niue over the summer of 1914–15 the most visible sign of war was the establishment and training of the 1st Niue Regiment. Three individuals played a leading role in this. Cornwall, the resident commissioner, had headed the New Zealand Administration on the island since his appointment in 1907, operating from the office attached to the residency in the centre of Alofi. While Cornwall had valuable financial and administrative skills, he also had a nasty temper and was feared by many; he was one of the reasons for the high turnover in administration staff sent to work in his office and in education, health and policing.

Relations between the resident commissioner and the LMS missionary in charge also deteriorated after Frank and Sarah Lawes departed. Reverend James Cullen, a new arrival to the island in 1914, inherited a prickly relationship between mission and administration, but he threw his weight and the influence of the church behind the drive to recruit a regiment. In a letter to Cornwall in November 1914 he wrote:

> the church will do everything in its power to encourage recruiting. [The regiment] may certainly drill on Church ground, providing that an undertaking

> is given that no drilling or congregation of men be allowed on the ground on Sunday, or during the hours of divine service during the week.[12]

The third key person in setting up the regiment was the chief of police, Sergeant Major Frederick Holmes, recently arrived in Niue from police duties in the Cook Islands. Holmes was a Londoner and had served in the British Army for 23 years, most of that time in the Coldstream Guards. He had seen service in India, China and South Africa and, as a seasoned drill sergeant, was keen to supervise training on the village green.

The Island Council, with representatives from all the villages, was also supportive of the idea of a Niue regiment. The elders encouraged young men to come forward as Sergeant Holmes, with assistance from the administration office, toured the island to recruit men. For a lot of young Niueans it was a chance not to be missed – to travel was to escape the isolation of Niue and the church-dominated society that had developed there over the previous 60 years; they could leave behind the onerous family, village and church obligations and the strictly enforced moral code, including a total alcohol ban for 'natives'. Some of the men who now enlisted had already experienced life beyond Niue on 12-month labour contracts and were quick to seize the opportunity for another adventure. One man later recalled how he and two others were on labour contracts in Samoa when war was declared and they saw the New Zealand troops arrive and seize the German territory. When they heard that a force was being raised in Niue they returned on an island freighter to sign up.[13]

Not everyone was keen to enlist, of course, and there is anecdotal evidence that some men took evasive action. When news spread that the recruiting team was approaching a village, men hid or even took their families and lived in the bush until the recruiters had moved on.[14] Other men who had initially enlisted, withdrew their names because the story went round that 'if you go to war you die and never come back to Niue'.[15] Ikimatatoa, one of the native mission teachers, preached at a service in November 1914 against participation in a war on the other side of the world. If a bullet went through a man's body in battle, he told the congregation, it would also go through his soul, thus disqualifying the victim from entering heaven. This dread fate, he explained, would only happen to those who went abroad to fight; if they waited until the enemy came to Niue and were killed in Niue, they would indeed be blessed.[16] Cullen confirmed that these words had been spoken in church and the sentiments were roundly condemned by Holmes in a letter to the resident commissioner. Nothing further was heard of Ikimatatoa.

Drilling soon began on the Alofi and Hakupu village greens, with 200–250 men involved in the training programme. Cornwall noted that 'drilling is in the air just now'[17] and Holmes huffed and puffed about his 'arduous and unthankful job of raising a native regiment'.[18] In truth he was probably thoroughly enjoying himself, using his drilling experience from his time at Aldershot, the main British Army training base in England; a later report noted that the Niue men had been learning 'Aldershot oaths' from their sergeant major.[19] In the absence of any equipment whatsoever, drilling – military marching to command – was the only training that could be carried out.

Niue Island's involvement in the Great War could well have ended there – with marching and drumming on the village green and contributing to patriotic funds in New Zealand. Activities such as these relieved the consciences of the Pālagi community who were anxious about relatives in England, and the drills were popular with the Islanders. Indeed, Cullen suggested this was as far as anyone anticipated the Niue Island involvement in the war would go. He wrote in January 1915: 'when news of the war reached Niue the people not only sent a money contribution but offered to send 200 men to fight. I do not for a moment suppose that the offer will be accepted …'[20] He thought it 'quite unlikely' the men would be called for service, and later in 1915 he noted, 'we had been hoping their services would not be required'.[21]

To understand why the New Zealand government eventually accepted the offer of troops from Niue it is necessary to look closely at the recruitment of Māori into the NZEF. Until 1914 the British government had refused to allow the use of 'coloured colonials' in active service alongside white troops. For this reason it had turned down New Zealand's offer to dispatch a Native Contingent to serve in the South African war of 1899–1902.

By 1914 the idea still did not sit comfortably with the British government or army authorities, and individuals within the United Kingdom who tried to enlist were met with refusal. Ratu Josefa Sukuna, a young Fijian chief who had been sent to Oxford in 1913 to study law, tried to enlist in 1914 but was 'utterly rejected by the British Army as a coloured man';[22] he crossed the Channel to France, enlisted in the French Foreign Legion and saw action on the Western Front for most of 1915 before he was invalided home to Fiji with bullet wounds to the head but also with the Croix de Guerre for bravery. The British authorities were also unwilling, at least at the outset of war, to accept indigenous troops from the colonies. They rejected offers from Fiji in 1915 to

Fiji Native Labour Corps visiting Stanley Park in Vancouver on their way to serve on the docks of Calais and Marseilles. The British authorities resisted offers of indigenous troops from Fiji until finally, in January 1917, they agreed to take a labour corps. Ratu Sukuna was made quartermaster sergeant of the Labour Corps. He was desperate for his fellow Fijians to have a fighting role but agreed to serve in any capacity. After the war this group was declared ineligible for payment of war gratuities. CITY OF VANCOUVER ARCHIVES, MIL P56 provide indigenous Fijians; they made it clear they would accept only 'men of pure European descent'.[23]

While they could reject individuals at the enlistment office and specify exactly who they were prepared to take from their colonies, it was more difficult for the British authorities to place conditions on offers of troops from the dominions – those senior members of the empire, including New Zealand, that had achieved a large measure of autonomy from Britain in the years preceding the Great War.[24] Britain retained control of overall foreign policy, including the ability to declare war independently, but the dominions had 'the autonomy to decide the scope of men and materials offered to the Imperial war effort'.[25]

Furthermore the British authorities soon realised that they would need far greater numbers of troops and support teams, equipment and supplies than they had ever imagined. Early on in the war Britain had set a precedent by using non-white troops from India. The Indian Army, which served the British authorities within India, was larger than the British Army itself in August 1914, and Indian units were immediately sent to the conflict on the Western Front. By the end of the war, over 1.3 million Indian troops had been involved, as infantry and as labour force.

In New Zealand, which had been a dominion since 1907, the indigenous Māori population enjoyed equality in law with Pākehā or Europeans, and representation in parliament in the general electorate seats and in four Māori electorate seats. By 1914 a new generation of Māori leaders had emerged, and they believed it was essential that Māori prove their loyalty and worth to Pākehā New Zealanders to achieve greater equality of opportunity. They pressed for Māori to be allowed to enlist and to form a distinct Maori Contingent. The minister of defence put this in an official request to the imperial government, which approved it in September 1914.

A Native Contingent Committee was set up to oversee the selection of men for the Maori Contingent. The committee consisted of the five Māori members of parliament – Maui Pomare, Apirana Ngata, Peter Buck and Taare Parata representing the four Māori electorates, and James Carroll, the only Māori to hold a general electorate seat. The committee chair, Pomare, was perhaps the most vocal in expressing his desire for Māori to play an active part in the war effort. There was no shortage of willing volunteers and, in February 1915, after they had trained in a temporary camp on the Avondale racecourse in Auckland, Pomare farewelled the 1st Maori Contingent of 500 men. They sailed for Egypt and then, in accordance with the agreement that the contingent would be used in a support role, they were deployed to Malta on garrison duty. With the escalation of events on the Gallipoli peninsula, however, the imperial government requested that the Maori Contingent be sent in on active service.

This created a problem that had not been seriously considered up to this point. An active role would involve injury and loss of life, and the contingent would need reinforcements. The Native Contingent Committee was keen for the men to see active service despite the fact that many iwi elders had agreed to participation in the belief that it would involve garrison duty only. The committee promised it could provide a reinforcement of around 350 men in October 1915 and another by the middle of February 1916. On the strength of this promise, the Maori Contingent was sent in to Gallipoli. In August 1915 the men were involved in action that won them high praise for their bravery, but in which more than 20 per cent of them were killed or wounded. General Sir Alexander Godley, commander of the New Zealand forces throughout the war, was now concerned about the size of the Maori Contingent and he was unhappy with the actions of some of the Māori officers on Gallipoli. He decided to split the Māori soldiers among battalions of the New Zealand infantry, and to send some of the officers back home.[26] These actions brought great protest from the committee, which considered it vital to retain the special identity of the Maori Contingent. The problem was resolved in February 1916 when the British authorities gave permission for the formation of a separate New Zealand Division. Godley now reorganised the whole New Zealand force. He needed a Pioneer Battalion – a labouring unit – and he decided to group all the Māori into that along with an equal number of Pākehā volunteers. All future Māori reinforcements would be posted to the Pioneer Battalion, and Godley hoped it would eventually become almost entirely a Māori unit.

Sikh and Gurkha soldiers at Gallipoli, 1915. New Zealand soldiers first encountered men from the Indian subcontinent in Egypt and at Gallipoli. Despite reservations about the use of non-white troops, British Army officials soon realised that the war was going to require a huge workforce and Indian units were rapidly brought in. By the end of the war 1.3 million Indians had served, both as infantry and as labourers. ALEXANDER TURNBULL LIBRARY, WELLINGTON, NEW ZEALAND, 1/2-077916-F

RIGHT: *The training of the New Zealand Native Contingent in late 1914. 'Scenes at Avondale, Auckland, where the Maori volunteers have been transformed into an efficient fighting force.' The caption in the* Auckland Weekly News *does not mention the fact that it had been agreed to use the Maori Contingent in a support role only.* SIR GEORGE GREY SPECIAL COLLECTIONS, AUCKLAND LIBRARIES, NEW ZEALAND, AWNS-19150218-37-1

1

2

3

4

5

6

7

8

11

Minister of Defence Sir James Allen tries to encourage Māori enlistment in the Waikato. Standing alongside him is Apirana Ngata, MP for Eastern Maori and a member of the Native Contingent Committee. Seated in the front row, visible between Ngata and Allen, is Dr Maui Pomare, MP for Western Maori, which included Waikato. Lack of support from this region for a foreign war was a key consideration in accepting the offer of troops from Niue and the Cook Islands. SIR GEORGE GREY SPECIAL COLLECTIONS, AUCKLAND LIBRARIES, NEW ZEALAND, AWNS-19161130-38-7

The latter part of 1915, before the creation of this Pioneer Battalion, proved a difficult time for the committee, and Pomare was placed in a particularly invidious position. There was growing opposition to sending more young Māori men away to fight as news was received of the losses on Gallipoli, the breakup of the Maori Contingent as a distinct unit, and the decision to return four of the Māori officers to New Zealand. Nowhere was that opposition stronger than in Pomare's own electorate of Western Māori – a section of the North Island that comprised principally Taranaki and the Waikato. These were the areas that, during the New Zealand Wars of the 1860s, had suffered the

Dr Maui Wiremu Pomare, later Sir Maui Pomare, member of parliament for Western Maori, minister for Cook and other Islands. ALEXANDER TURNBULL LIBRARY, WELLINGTON, NEW ZEALAND, 1/1-014581-G

humiliation of defeat and also the confiscation of hundreds of thousands of hectares of their best land. They were not now prepared to offer their young men to fight a European war on the other side of the world. Other districts shared these sentiments. Ngāpuhi in the north drew up a petition to the governor-general in early 1916 in which they stated that such recruitment was against the spirit of 'a sacred treaty,' the Treaty of Waitangi, drawn up under 'the mana of our mother, Queen Victoria', to protect the Māori race. Sending one contingent of 500 men was 'sufficient to evidence their faith' and, given the overall number of Māori, 'the proportion was equally sufficient'.[27]

Fortunately Pomare had one other political card to play to fulfil the promise to supply two groups of reinforcements. He was the first Māori member of parliament to hold cabinet rank as 'representative of the Native Race and minister responsible for the Cook and other Islands' – a portfolio he had held since 1912 and had been reassigned in the wartime cabinet set up in December 1914. As the issue of Māori reinforcements began to appear very difficult, the

Sir James Allen, minister of defence 1912–20. ALEXANDER TURNBULL LIBRARY, WELLINGTON, NEW ZEALAND, 1/1-001203-G

minister of defence, James Allen, began discussing with Pomare the possibility of accepting troop offers from the Cook Islands and Niue.

Initial requests from Pomare to Allen to consider the Niue offer of troops were made early in 1915. 'The people of Niue are anxious that the services of their Contingent should be availed of in some manner and I should be glad to know whether anything can be done in this direction.'[28] Allen's response was emphatic:

> I regret there is no way in which a Contingent of Natives of Niue Island could be utilised for overseas service. At the same time, it would be as well to convey to the Islanders our appreciation of their patriotic action and we will rely on them … for the defence of the Island of Niue in the case of an attack or raid by the enemy.[29]

At this stage the Maori Contingent had just left New Zealand en route to Egypt and the idea of future reinforcements was not under consideration. By the end of June 1915 the situation had changed. The Maori Contingent had moved to a combatant role on Gallipoli and reinforcements had been promised. Allen wrote again to Pomare:

> I would suggest that the question of now accepting recruits from Cook and Niue Islands be considered, especially if there is any difficulty in securing in New Zealand the number required for the Maori Reinforcements.[30]

That sentence was a barb to Pomare. His mana was threatened by opposition to enlistment in his Western Maori electorate, but as minister for the Cook and other Islands he could take some credit for the participation of Pacific recruits. As one writer described it, 'these two groups were in a sense Pomare's Own'.[31]

Forty-five men recruited from the Cook Islands arrived in Wellington in early October and were welcomed in the parliamentary debating chamber by the minister of defence and members of the Native Contingent Committee. The 'South Sea Islanders' responded in song. Meanwhile Pomare, now a captain in the New Zealand army, sailed to Niue in October 1915 to accompany the Niue Islanders to New Zealand as their commanding officer. He had been embarrassed by the lack of support in his own electorate; the acceptance of Islanders to fill the ranks of the Maori Contingent was a way round a political impasse.

Scene at the recruiting office in Alofi, September 1915. Families came from around Niue to see if their men were accepted for enlistment into the army. They are dressed in their best clothes as they wait patiently in front of the missionary residence. One young man, at the bottom centre of the photo, is wearing an army cap, confirmation that he has been enlisted.
COURTESY OF RICHARD HOLDEN, CHRISTCHURCH

CHAPTER 3

Departure from Niue

When the London Missionary Society vessel *John Williams* arrived to inspect the mission station at Alofi on 29 September 1915, the village was abuzz with activity. Two days earlier a ship had arrived from New Zealand with army medical personnel on board and the news that the men from Niue were going to war. Instructions were to carry out the examination of recruits before the arrival of a troopship. The LMS report stated that 'enthusiastic recruiting was going on, two hundred of the natives having volunteered to go to the war, about 140 of whom had already passed the doctor, and were, in a few days, about to leave for New Zealand to go into camp for training'.[1]

On board the mission vessel was Dr Carl H. Seaforth from Sydney, the new medical officer for the New Zealand Administration. There had been no doctor on Niue since March 1915 when Dr J.P. Cameron, a 29-year-old Scotsman who had been on the island for six months, had 'died with extreme suddenness'.[2] Seaforth was already known to Niueans as he had come to the island as the first medical officer in 1911 under his original name, Schumacher. He had returned to New Zealand in September 1912. The official reason for this early departure was ill health but it is likely that Schumacher had clashed with the resident commissioner, Henry Cornwall, and had been forced to leave.[3] When war broke out in 1914 the Schumachers changed their name to Seaforth to avoid the backlash common for people with German names;[4] Cornwall had no doubt agreed to the appointment of the new medical officer without realising Schumacher and Seaforth were one and the same man. Seaforth stayed on Niue long enough to assist with medical examinations and to sign most of the medical certificates for the recruits but when the troopship departed he was on board and Niue was once again without a doctor. When Cornwall was interviewed on a visit to New Zealand in early 1916 he commented that Niueans 'have no time for Germans – absolutely no time'[5]. It was more likely that Cornwall had no time for an official who had stood up to him previously.

The recruiting office had been set up in Alofi in what was normally the customs bond store. It was centrally placed near the main church, the office of the resident commissioner, the home of the resident missionary and the wharf. Captain Arnold Izard, surgeon in the New Zealand Medical Corps, had arrived with other medical personnel. He was sent to Niue because he had earlier served as medical advisor to the King of Tonga and, more recently, as medical officer with the Samoan Relief Force. This was a feature of New Zealand army decisions concerning the Pacific Island recruits: there was a real effort to find and deploy men who had some Pacific connection or experience that might help ease their way.

In an article published in Auckland papers, Seaforth explained the process that ensued in Alofi.[6] The recruits underwent a medical examination and those that passed were then formally enlisted into the NZEF: this involved filling in the attestation papers and taking the oath of allegiance to King George V. Many of the men did not speak English, so the process of enlistment was lengthy. Each question on the attestation paper had to be read out then translated into Vagahau Niue; the recruit's answer was translated back into English and recorded on the form. The men who were nonliterate made a mark on the paper, and the signature or mark had to be witnessed and signed off. There was no official record of births, deaths and marriages on Niue so birthdates were often sketchy. If there was any doubt, the year 1895 was recorded as this meant the man was legally old enough to join the army.

Seaforth later described the activity and excitement. People from the resident commissioner's office and from the ship were busy helping to fill in the papers. The recruits were accompanied by family who had all come together to Alofi from around the island: a considerable crowd gathered around the recruiting office to see who was accepted and who was rejected. Officers from the ship called out height and weight measurements, then the doctor examined the men and signed the certificate of medical examination. Those accepted were classed malolō, good; they then proceeded to the desk to complete the enlistment papers. Most of the papers were witnessed by Joseph McMahon-Box, a young official who had joined the resident commissioner's staff earlier in 1915. He was assisted by Sergeant Ihaia Kingi of Gisborne, who had enlisted for the Maori Contingent and would serve in the same reinforcements as the men from Niue. Finally the recruit stood to take the oath, witnessed by Cornwall. When the process was complete, the man was given an army cap 'as a confirmation that he was passed and confirmed a soldier'.[7] Seaforth reported that all this activity went on with great haste as they were expecting the troopship bearing Pomare, minister for the Cook and other Islands and, once it arrived, all men had to be ready to board for a quick departure. As men completed the process and received their cap they returned to their respective villages to await the arrival of the troopship.

The absence of any regular shipping service was a major problem in bringing the Niue recruits to Auckland. In order to collect the Niue men the Army Department tried to divert a steamer on the Samoa–Fiji–Auckland run but the request was turned down; the shipping company needed to get 1000 cases of bananas and 350 cases of tomatoes to market as soon as possible. Instead the government had to charter a vessel to collect the Niue recruits. The agreement with the Union Steam Ship Company to charter SS *Te Anau* cost the Army Department £2000 – more than double the cost of getting Cook Islanders to New Zealand on a regular service from Tahiti to Auckland.[8] Cost was an ongoing factor in bringing men from the Pacific, as the Army Department realised that at some point their return passage would also need to be arranged and paid for.

Te Anau was sighted approaching Niue on 12 October 1915 and the call went out around the island. Because there was no radio communication with the outside world there was always a scramble when a vessel was spotted. Messengers were dispatched to all the villages with orders for the enlisted men to gather in Alofi ready for departure the next day. The recruitment process had not been completed and some men were only partly processed before departure. Their attestation papers show that the weighing machine had already been packed and medical examinations were cursory, to say the least. This detail surfaced in Auckland when some of those hastily recruited were found to have long-standing injuries that ruled them out of military service. The formal enlistment and swearing in of the final recruits had to wait until the men were at sea and the papers were signed by Dr Pomare himself.

The presence of Pomare on board caused a considerable stir of activity in Alofi. During his brief visit he entertained some of the island officials on board HMNZT *Te Anau* as it drifted out in the bay, unable to berth or to anchor. Villagers around the island prepared feasts to farewell their sons, and early the next morning families accompanied them from the outlying villages to Alofi. There was a parade on the Alofi green where Pomare inspected the men, accompanied by Holmes and Cornwall. A service was then held in the Alofi church, which was so full that the congregation spilled out onto the surrounding grass. Reverend Cullen later wrote to the LMS that this was only the second time Cornwall had attended church; the previous time was on the occasion of Pomare's visit in 1914. Cornwall had been on Niue since 1907 but he and the LMS were often locked in dispute and he had avoided church as much as possible.

Early in 1915 Cullen had written to the minister for the Cook and other Islands to offer his services as chaplain: 'in the event of the Niue Contingent being called to the front, I shall esteem it an honour to be allowed to accompany them as chaplain'.[9] He was disappointed that his offer was not accepted and, furthermore, that a Niuean 'ex-pastor', Uea, had been appointed instead. Cullen considered that Uea was 'not at all the man I should have chosen myself, and one I hardly think fitted for the post. But I was not consulted at all.'[10]

It appears from Cullen's letters that he was having marital problems and, as a result, Mrs Cullen and their two daughters had returned to England. He also had financial problems, and saw the higher pay of an army chaplain as a part solution to this. He blamed his rejection on Cornwall, and assumed that the reason for it could only be his age. Uea, the man who became chaplain, was a highly respected Niuean who had trained for the ministry on Niue under the Reverend Frank Lawes and had served as pastor of Alofi for nearly 20 years

After the farewell church service, families gathered above the wharf to watch the men embark in boats sent in from Te Anau, *which was lying out in Alofi Bay. Reverend Cullen later wrote, 'they went off in good spirits, and there was no wailing or excessive lamentation'.*
COURTESY OF RICHARD HOLDEN, CHRISTCHURCH

On the day of departure, 13 October 1915, the men of the Niue contingent line up on the village green in front of the New Zealand residency. They are inspected by Captain Pomare; he is followed by Dr Seaforth and Dr Izard, who have been responsible for examining the men and deciding who is fit for service. Another member of the medical team, Corporal Fisher, brings up the rear. COURTESY OF RICHARD HOLDEN, CHRISTCHURCH

before he retired in 1911 – hence Cullen's reference to him as an ex-pastor. Despite his disappointment Cullen carried out his duties as LMS missionary in charge on Niue. He conducted the farewell service and issued a copy of the Niuean New Testament to each member of the contingent. No bibles had been available for the previous three years but Frank Lawes had organised a new printing from London. Partly funded by Robert Henry Head, a prominent trader on Niue and staunch supporter of the LMS, the bibles had only just been delivered by the *John Williams* two weeks earlier. Cullen noted in a letter to Sarah Lawes that it would be 'a rather cumbersome volume for them to carry about with them but there is nothing smaller'.[11] Robert Head hoped 'the New Testaments you give to the men will be a blessing to them and a comfort at all times'.[12]

Captain Pomare entertained island officials on board HMNZT Te Anau *on 12 October 1915. He is standing on the left of the photo in his military uniform. Clockwise from Pomare is Mr W. Prosser, first mate of* Te Anau, *Captain Baron, master of* Te Anau, *Dr Arnold Izard of the New Zealand Medical Corps and Henry Cornwall, resident commissioner on Niue.* COURTESY OF RICHARD HOLDEN, CHRISTCHURCH

After the service there was more feasting and speechmaking by 'the older men and wise ones of the island',[13] more uniform items were issued and then, late in the day, the embarkation began. *Te Anau* lay half a mile offshore, and families gathered on the cliffs above the wharf to watch each group being rowed out to the troopship. Men launched vaka and accompanied the row-boats out into the bay. Cullen wrote to Sarah Lawes, 'they went off in good spirits, and there was no wailing or excessive lamentation. May GOD guard them and bring them back soon.'[14] Seaforth, in his reporting for the Auckland papers, waxed lyrical:

> The morale was as good as that of old, seasoned and travelled troops. They [were] singing their native songs in their deep, manly voices … These poetical, yet extremely practical people are already soldiers in spirit, as they eagerly obey all the orders of the sergeants commanding them. They embark on the ship and Tommy Fiapa[15] is now a soldier on his way to camp in New Zealand.[16]

The reality for the men leaving and for the families standing on the cliffs watching was very different from the poetical description given by Cullen and Seaforth. For the men who embarked the excitement and adventure of a long voyage to unknown lands was tempered by the reality of leaving their island home and families – many for the first time.

For those who remained the prospect was equally bleak. Almost 50 per cent of the contingent were married; 30 left behind families of one to four children. Fives wives were pregnant.[17] One family from Hikutavake farewelled four sons: Hemu, Hipa, Peni and Pulu. At least seven families farewelled two sons each – Falaoa and Fasene from Avatele; Finiki and Lavaika, Likatau and Patuki, Lui and Vasau from Alofi; Pimeleko and Talauta, Mitikoni and Puhotau from Mutalau; Fanavai and Pieti from Lakepa. People on Niue tell the story of a headcount being conducted on the ship and when it was discovered there were 149 men, Pomare called for one more volunteer. No one wanted to join but eventually Peki Matagitakai, a policeman in Alofi, agreed to go. When his wife, Tapola of Hakupu, heard he had gone she swam out towards the ship to say goodbye. There were many tears and much sadness.[18]

One of the boats from Te Anau *alongside the troopship. As the members of the Niue contingent were rowed out to the troopship they were accompanied by locals in their vaka.*
COURTESY OF RICHARD HOLDEN, CHRISTCHURCH

A group of Niueans, mainly children, watch the soldiers departing.
COURTESY OF RICHARD HOLDEN, CHRISTCHURCH

The lack of any system of communication other than the irregular steamer service meant the wait for news must have been hard to bear. All this was on top of an already difficult year that had begun with a devastating cyclone,[19] followed by a drought and food shortages. Life on Niue was never easy, and now a large portion of the young, able-bodied men had gone. Much of the coconut crop that provided income from copra had been destroyed by the cyclone; imported goods were unobtainable or too expensive on account of the war; food crops were scarce because of the drought. Furthermore the cyclone season was fast approaching, which meant even fewer visits by trading vessels with the possibility of news of the war or – more importantly now – news of the Niue contingent.

Members of the Niue contingent on board Te Anau, *en route for Auckland. Uniform items were distributed during the voyage; the man standing on the left displays a shoe.*
COURTESY OF RICHARD HOLDEN, CHRISTCHURCH

DETAIL: *No. 4 Niue Platoon of the 3rd Maori Reinforcements.*
ALEXANDER TURNBULL LIBRARY, WELLINGTON, NEW ZEALAND, 1/2-042997/F

CHAPTER 4

Training at Narrow Neck

After a very rough passage to New Zealand, SS *Te Anau*, bearing the Niue Island contingent, berthed at Calliope Wharf in Devonport on 19 October 1915. Many of the men had suffered badly from seasickness during the voyage and the sight of land was a relief to them all. During the voyage more uniform items had been issued so that, when they arrived in New Zealand, they were dressed in denim trousers and jackets, forage caps and military overcoats. Among their personal belongings they brought Niuean crafts – pandanus fans and baskets, model canoes, polished shells and necklaces – that they hoped to sell for some extra money. Members of the small Niuean community already resident in Auckland were waiting on the wharf to greet the new arrivals. Once they had disembarked the men were lined up and, with Sergeant Holmes accompanying them, set off marching through Devonport to their new home: Narrow Neck military camp. As the *New Zealand Herald* reported:

> practically none of these islanders had seen anything resembling a town before. Everything was new and strange to them [and] … they were naturally anxious to stare at such things as ferry boats and motor buses and three-storey buildings and Devonport's modest, verandahed street …[1]

Narrow Neck, or Nalo Neke as the Niuean men called it, was one of the camps hastily constructed after the outbreak of war to train reinforcements before they were sent to the Middle East and, later, France. It was an area of crown land where Fort Takapuna was built in the 1880s during a Russian invasion scare. A new camp had been constructed there, designed to become permanent army barracks. It was small, as military camps went – it held only 400 men, compared to Trentham camp, which housed 4500. The camp sat on a narrow isthmus linking Devonport to Takapuna, just above Narrow Neck beach, with a view out across the Waitemata Harbour to Rangitoto Island.

While the Narrow Neck camp was being built the Maori Contingent had trained at a makeshift camp at Avondale Racecourse. Future Māori reinforcements would be trained at Narrow Neck camp – perhaps out of a fear that new recruits might have typhoid and would need to be kept isolated from other troops. The district health officer in Auckland was worried that 'carriers' would be impossible to trace before they spread the disease. James Allen urged that all recruits be inoculated, and eventually made it compulsory for the Maori Contingent.[2] By the time the Niueans and Cook Islanders arrived, the Tunnelling Company reinforcements were also training at Narrow Neck and all men were inoculated as part of the preparation for overseas departure.

It was fortunate that the Niueans were assigned to a small training camp. Several difficulties soon became apparent, some of which could have been worse if the men had been stationed in one of the large camps where there were more men in training than the entire population of Niue. The most immediate problem was language. One report stated that only one of the Niueans spoke English; in fact, 10 or 12 of them had some knowledge of English and Holmes also had 'a knowledge of the island language' – but probably only sufficient for basic communication. Uea, who had been appointed chaplain, had a good working knowledge of English, as did Fasene, who gave his occupation on

The Niuean men training at Nalo Neke camp on the North Shore, a week after their arrival. The caption read: 'Sturdy Niue Island recruits ... now in training for the front'. SIR GEORGE GREY SPECIAL COLLECTIONS, AUCKLAND LIBRARIES, NEW ZEALAND, AWNS-19151028-46-5

enlistment as 'pupil teacher' –he had been taught by his father Tosene, the mission teacher in the village of Avatele. Hipa had served as a mission teacher with the LMS in New Guinea, where English was the lingua franca. Other men had been on labour contracts or had crewed on vessels and had no doubt had some exposure to English, although contract labourers were often kept in a group with one person acting as translator.

At Narrow Neck, Fasene was recognised as the interpreter for the Niueans. The men were organised into groups according to the village they came from; villages were then paired, and one person from each group was appointed to take charge. Holmes, assisted by Fasene, selected these men, mainly on their ability with language. Some villages had no English speakers; others, in particular Alofi, had several, and they were put in charge of other village groupings. Each group was allocated a hut where they set up quarters. The appointment of non-commissioned officers – sergeants, corporals and lance corporals – was left until 1 January 1916 when a number of officers were appointed. These were men who had English language skills and who, by now, had had some leadership experience; half of them were from Alofi.

The army made an effort to appoint commissioned officers – positions reserved for Europeans – who had some experience of the Pacific. One young officer was already known to some of the men: Second Lieutenant Archibald MacDonald had worked in Niue as a customs officer before the outbreak of war. He had left Niue suddenly in 1915 after a major disagreement with Cornwall. His departure was put down to ill health, but MacDonald enlisted for military service almost immediately. He was en route to the Middle East when preparations were being made to bring the Niuean contingent to Auckland for training. When Pomare learnt of a young officer who had spent time on Niue he asked the minister of defence to bring MacDonald back to New Zealand and place him with the 3rd Maori Reinforcements: 'knowing something of the Niuean language and the characteristics of the men I think it would be advisable to appoint him if possible, especially as he was very popular among the Natives of Niue'.[3] MacDonald was taken from the troopship when it reached Albany in southwest Australia and returned to Narrow Neck in time

Niueans on the parade ground. Footwear was a particular problem for men from Niue – they had always gone barefoot over the hard coral surface of the island and now they had to wear boots, or shoes as an interim measure.
SIR GEORGE GREY SPECIAL COLLECTIONS, AUCKLAND LIBRARIES, NEW ZEALAND, 7-A14272

for the arrival of the Niueans. He trained with them at Narrow Neck and later travelled with them to Egypt, France and England before returning to New Zealand with some of the group.[4]

Two other young men were appointed junior officers with the Niuean group – George Fromm and Alexander Melles. They had no previous experience in the Pacific but they trained with the Niuean men and travelled with them to Egypt. Fromm, like MacDonald, went on with the Niueans to France and England and back to New Zealand; he then returned to the Middle East to serve with the Rarotongan Company.[5]

Two days after the Niueans arrived at Nalo Neke they were visited by Brigadier General A.W. Robin, commandant general of the New Zealand forces, and Surgeon General R. Henderson, director general of medical services. The men were already undergoing drilling at the camp and learning commands such as 'right', 'left', 'about turn' and 'stand easy'. Robin commented: 'the camp is a little Tower of Babel. The language difficulty is a very real one at present'.[6] Another report noted that the Rarotongan group was training with the Māori recruits and they all got along more easily than did the Māori with the Niue

Islanders, 'due to the difference in language and temperament'.[7] This was perhaps a reflection of the difference in cultures – the New Zealand Māori language and culture are closer to those of the Cook Islands than of Niue.

Henderson noted another problem for the Niueans: footwear. They had never worn footwear of any kind, so it was very difficult for them to fit on army boots and march for hours at a stretch. A reporter who accompanied the senior army personnel to the camp observed:

> Some wore boots. A larger number favoured slippers of brown leather without heels. One … had one boot off and one boot on. The man in all the squad who moved most easily marched over the scoria surface without a covering for his feet. Nearly all the Niueans have lived for 20 years or more without boots. Their feet are huge, covered with masses of muscle … those … who have found boots to fit them in the camp stores have developed sore feet, and are awkward and profoundly unhappy.[8]

The camp commandant, Captain Peacock, decided to have boots made specially for the Niueans, and Henderson, who knew the problems ill-fitting boots would cause, stressed that care would need to be taken with measurement and fitting; one man's feet, he observed, were 12.5 inches (31.75cm) long.

Food was another problem for the Niueans in training. The food issued in the camp, with a heavy emphasis on meat, was very different from the usual island diet and was making the men ill. The *Auckland Weekly News* reported one particular incident when half the Niueans were struck down with stomach pain and vomiting.[9] One of the men recalled later that 'the cook poisoned the rice' and 'the animal flesh was not cooked'.[10] Normal army rations were adjusted to give the Niueans and Cook Islanders considerably less meat and more fish and fruit:

> Their morning meal generally includes boiled rice, with peaches, apricots or pineapples, and the principal meal of the day contains meat three or four times a week, but generally meat is replaced with large quantities of fresh fish … Large quantities of potatoes and other vegetables, and piles of bread and butter, make up the menu.[11]

In late November 1915 James Allen visited the men at Narrow Neck camp. He reported to his colleagues in parliament and also wrote to the commander of the New Zealand Expeditionary Force in Egypt to express concern about the food and clothing, especially the boots. He told members of parliament: 'They are a fine lot of men but there are great difficulties encountered in fitting them for active service. They are not accustomed to this kind of life – not accustomed to boots, and not accustomed to military food.'[12] To his military commander in the field, Allen mused: 'I do not quite see how you will get on with them when we send them to you. Perhaps it may be better to keep them together in garrison duty somewhere.'[13]

The community back in Niue was without further news until mid-December 1915, when a vessel arrived bringing news that the men had reached New Zealand safely and were in training; and returning five of the men because of illness. Cullen commented in a letter: 'five [men] have already been returned, sick from the bad weather and cold. Our boys need heat, and the sooner they get to Egypt or Turkey the better it will be for them.'[14]

This first group of men who were declared medically unfit for service in November 1915 were suffering from a number of complaints, and at least three had conditions that should have excluded them from enlistment in the first place. Their medical records reveal how cursory the checks were on Niue. One man passed inspection in Alofi with 'lungs normal' and, despite the observation that he had 'one finger useless due to old crush by machinery', Pomare had added during the voyage to New Zealand that the soldier would still be able 'to pull a rifle trigger'. The medical board in Auckland thought differently: it found he had tuberculosis of the lung and was not fit for service. Another man was found unfit for service because of a stiff, painful shoulder that had troubled him for years after 'a fall from a tree'. Two others underwent hospital treatment in Auckland for what were described as 'chronic conditions' and were then discharged.[15] Another six men became ill and were discharged from service in Auckland in 1916. They received hospital treatment; three were discharged in April and three in June, and all were returned to the island.

One man, Private Vilipate of Liku, 22 years of age, was admitted to Narrow Neck camp hospital on 15 December with double pneumonia and, on Christmas Day 1915, became the first Niuean to die while enlisted in the

16/1371 Purie Davi Harry: a studio portrait taken in Auckland of Puleua from Liku. He had been working in New Zealand before the war began and had taken an anglicised name. He enlisted in January 1916 and was added to the Niuean group already in training at Narrow Neck. SIR GEORGE GREY SPECIAL COLLECTIONS, AUCKLAND LIBRARIES, NEW ZEALAND, 31-H2290 (H.J. SCHMIDT)

NZEF. On 27 December his body was placed on a gun carriage drawn by four horses and conveyed to O'Neills Point cemetery, not far from the camp. Chaplain Uea conducted the service, Niue men provided the firing party and, at the end of the service, the Last Post was sounded. News of his death did not reach Niue for five months. Several newspapers in New Zealand carried reports of Vilipate's death but they all reported him as Private Adipa.[16] Niuean names were mispronounced and misspelt throughout the war, and Niue and the Cook Islands were regularly confused in newspapers and in official documents.

Although the Niuean group lost some of their men to illness, four more Niueans joined in December and January. Two men who had been working as contract labourers in Tonga arrived in Auckland in late December and enlisted. Lauho, who had been employed as a wharf labourer in Nuku`alofa, enlisted at Narrow Neck on 20 December and a few days later an older man, 34-year-old Fata, was accepted for service. Both had been away from Niue for over two years and had accepted passage to New Zealand instead of the previously agreed passage back to Niue at the end of their labour contract. On 4 January 1916 a third Niuean, Puleua from Liku, arrived in camp; he had been working as a cook and handyman in hotels in Auckland and Hamilton for about three years. Puleua's name had changed over time as he realised it was usual in New Zealand to have at least a first name and a family name; he enlisted as Purie Davi Harry (the Harry was possibly borrowed from his employer, Harry Douglas of Hamilton). The final addition to the Niue group was Pauhumoana, the older brother of Puleua,[17] who was enlisted at Narrow Neck in late January 1916. It is likely he was the man who arrived on the ketch *Kereru* with Cornwall and his wife; the Auckland papers mentioned 'one recruit to join native camp'.[18] Although his late enlistment meant Pauhumoana had very little training before departure, the authorities probably thought it important to keep him with the Niuean group.

Many New Zealanders were interested and curious about the presence of the Niuean soldiers in Auckland: the men were seen as exotic, and were a great opportunity for journalists and photographers. The Auckland papers carried several articles and photos about the Niueans and their progress. The writing revealed a lack of knowledge about the Pacific in general, and Niue in particular; most were unsure exactly where Niue was, and unclear as to the relationship between Niue and New Zealand. The island was almost always regarded as part of the Cook Islands and was described variously as being in the South Seas, the inner Pacific and under British rule.

Stories in the press also revealed stereotypes that were commonly held about Pacific Islanders. For example, when the Niueans arrived in Auckland, people were surprised that the men had been seasick during the voyage. One writer noted, 'the Niue men ... are great sailors and famous as builders of canoes. Half their life is spent out on the heaving water ... they are half-amphibian in their capacity to swim long distances.'[19] There was no understanding that access to the sea is very difficult in Niue and that, unlike many other Pacific islands, there is no shallow lagoon and protective reef; as a consequence, many Niueans have never learnt to swim.

During their time in Auckland the Niueans were often involved in patriotic fundraising activities around the city, as citizens contributed enthusiastically to the war effort:

> The patriotic societies used any means at their disposal to induce donations. They held sports events, art unions (lotteries) and concerts ... They sold food and handcrafts at street stalls, and organised massive carnivals, with stalls, sideshows, raffles, food, dancing and singing culminating in the naming of a carnival queen – often the young woman whose supporters had raised the most money. Urban residents often had a wide choice of events and activities on which to spend their patriotic pounds.[20]

The presence of Pacific Island troops in their midst was an opportunity not to be missed. In late 1915 the Auckland Soldiers' Queen Committee organised events that featured the Niueans and Cook Islanders and their appearance was advertised as an obvious drawcard to the event. One event was held at

TOP: *The march from the training camp to Narrow Neck beach for a swim.* MIDDLE: *Swimming scene captioned as 'Merry Maoris and Niue Islanders'.* BOTTOM: *Men in the water at Narrow Neck beach. The buildings of the training camp can be seen on the headland behind.* SIR GEORGE GREY SPECIAL COLLECTIONS, AUCKLAND LIBRARIES, NEW ZEALAND, 7-A14558, 7-A14559, 7-A14560

Narrow Neck camp in late October. The campgrounds were decorated 'on a very enterprising and lavish scale'.[21] There were stalls selling fruit, flowers, sweets and fancy goods, a large refreshments tent, singing and dancing by the Cook Islanders and Niueans, entertainment by a military band, and a tug of war between the Pacific Islanders and the Tunnelling Company. In the evening movies were shown. In November the Soldiers' Queen Committee organised a Grand Moonlight Concert cruise on the Waitemata Harbour with onboard entertainment including singing and dancing by Rarotongans and Niue Islanders: the return fare from Devonport wharf was one shilling.

A military fête at Auckland Domain in November included the largest parade of men seen since war had been declared over a year earlier. 'The Niue Islanders, from the training camp at Narrow Neck, received a magnificent ovation as they swung by in their service kit.'[22] It seems the Pacific men were in demand, and these events provided new experiences and entertainment for them. They also attended services at the Newton Congregational Church, and their attendance was advertised in the church notices.

When Christmas arrived, special arrangements were made for the Niuean troops. The smaller group of Cook Island men were invited down to Rotorua and many of the Māori recruits were given leave to return home, but the Niuean men stayed in camp. After parade at 8am there was a church service, then a group of Devonport women arranged an 'appetising Christmas dinner … and the men did full justice to the repast'.[23] In the afternoon all were granted leave except the few needed on sentry duty and fatigues. The next day most of the Niue men were transported across the harbour to a picnic in the grounds of the Hon. George Fowlds' property at Mt Albert. Fowlds was a former MP and a strong supporter of the Congregational Church, and church members were present and assisted with refreshments and entertainment. The Niueans were the special guests of the day: they joined in enthusiastically in the sports events, and 'danced native dances and sang native songs' to thank the organisers.[24] The following day was the funeral for Private Vilipate, and on New Year's Eve His Excellency the Governor, the Earl of Liverpool, accompanied by his wife, the Countess of Liverpool, visited Narrow Neck to inspect the Niuean and Rarotongan contingents.

No. 4 Niue Platoon of the 3rd Maori Reinforcements – an official photo taken at Narrow Neck camp. There would have been three platoons of Niueans but this is the only official photo to have been found. Sergeant Uea, appointed chaplain to the group, is sitting in the centre of the front row. ALEXANDER TURNBULL LIBRARY, WELLINGTON, NEW ZEALAND, 1/2-042997/F

Above all, the participation of the Niueans served to reinforce the very patriotic notion of 'empire' that was such a vital ingredient in the general thinking of New Zealanders at this time – and in the support they were prepared to give Britain in the war. The fact that men from 'the furthest isles of the world's greatest ocean have heard the call to war'[25] was surely proof of the extent of the British Empire and the recognition by all who lived within its realms that it was something worth fighting for:

> If the Great War was an education to white men, how much more so to these South Sea Islanders to whom everything appeared so strange and wonderful. No finer proof of the strength and extent of British rule has ever been afforded than was given by these Islanders, who sacrificed everything to serve an Empire, the fairness and justice of whose rule they had learnt to appreciate.[26]

Full kit parade of Māori and Niue Island soldiers at Narrow Neck camp prior to departure for Egypt on 4 February 1916. SIR GEORGE GREY SPECIAL COLLECTIONS, AUCKLAND LIBRARIES, NEW ZEALAND, 7-A14562

By late January 1916 the training programme was nearing completion. The men had received some instruction in handling weapons, constructing trenches, general army procedures and following instructions in English. Private Puleoti recalled with pride an incident when he and Private Lukupa were on guard duty at an entrance gate and gave the correct command, 'Halt, your pass please!' to someone who turned out to be an officer. He was pleased with their performance and congratulated them: 'the Niue soldiers are quick to learn … and should now go to the front line'.[27] The men from Niue were readied for departure as part of the 3rd Maori Reinforcements. They were being sent to Egypt to help bolster the numbers in the New Zealand Expeditionary Force, which was heavily reduced in strength after the Gallipoli campaign of 1915. A convoy of vessels was preparing to sail with 1500 troops – the 3rd Maori Reinforcements, the 4th Battalion of the New Zealand Rifle Brigade and

sections A and D of the New Zealand Rifle Brigade Field Ambulance. All were to assemble in Auckland on Friday 4 February 1916 for the farewell.

Every departure of troops from New Zealand was the occasion for a militaryspectacle and an outpouring of patriotic fervour. It must have been a stirring event for all involved but perhaps all the more so for the men from Niue, who were unused to such crowds. A march was to take place through the city followed by a gathering in the Auckland Domain, where the governor of New Zealand, Lord Liverpool, the mayor of Auckland, the minister of defence and the minister for the Cook and other Islands would address the troops. Bad weather on the morning meant a change in plans: the march was limited to the length of Queen Street, and the speeches were held in front of the Town Hall. The mayor had declared a half-day holiday: shops and offices were closed, and Queen Street was lined with a dense mass of spectators. Mounted constables cleared a passage for the soldiers through the crowds. It was a proud moment for the Niueans:

Boarding the transport vessel Navua *at Queens Wharf. The caption referred to 'the dusky troops embarking' and described them as Māori and Niue Island troops.* SIR GEORGE GREY SPECIAL COLLECTIONS, AUCKLAND LIBRARIES, NEW ZEALAND, AWNS-19160224-43-2

> The Maori contingent – in this instance members of the branch of their race that hails from Rarotonga and from distant Niue Island – were splendid specimens of humanity. The men in the front ranks of each of their companies might be described as giants – huge, six-foot men, and broad-shouldered in proportion. With bayonets fixed, and their rifles at the slope, and distinguished from the rest by wearing overcoats and helmets, they strode along the street with an expression of imperturbability on each countenance, their military bearing comparing most creditably with that of their European comrades.[28]

The military parade was followed by speeches and then refreshments provided by the Women's Patriotic League. Each of the speakers referred to the presence of Pacific Islanders in the New Zealand forces, but as there were no interpreters many of the men were unaware they had been mentioned. Nevertheless, they shared in the importance of the occasion, and the crowds

Departure parade of 1500 troops along Queen Street, Auckland, on 4 February 1916.
SIR GEORGE GREY SPECIAL COLLECTIONS, AUCKLAND LIBRARIES, NEW ZEALAND, AWNS-19160210-35-2

DETAIL: *No. 4 Niue Platoon of the 3rd Maori Reinforcements.*
ALEXANDER TURNBULL LIBRARY, WELLINGTON, NEW ZEALAND, 1/2-042997/F

and the cheering accompanied them as they made their way to the wharf for embarkation.

The Māori reinforcements sailed on SS *Navua*, renamed for war purposes His Majesty's New Zealand Troopship No. 44. The total group of Māori reinforcements consisted of 140 Niue Islanders, 115 Māori, 45 Cook Islanders and six other men with Pacific Island connections who had individually applied for enlistment and been included in this reinforcement. Kaipati was from the Gilbert and Ellice Islands and was an experienced police constable.[29] Sione Taliauli, from Tonga, was studying medicine in New Zealand when he enlisted; he later died of pneumonia in Palestine in the last month of the war. Francis and Baisley Leger were brothers from Tonga.[30] Edward Westbrook, from Samoa, was the son of George Westbrook, a well-known English trader and planter who had come to the Pacific in the 1870s, married a Wallis Islander and eventually settled in Samoa where he became a member of the Legislative Council. Frank Payn, born in Tonga of an English father and a Tongan mother, was working in New Zealand when he decided to enlist.

There were two other transport ships in the convoy as it left Auckland: SS *Mokoia* and SS *Ulimaroa*. The Niuean men were now truly on their way. From this point on they would always be part of a much bigger group – and often bewildered because they did not understand English. We can only imagine the mix of emotions they felt as they embarked on the five-week journey to war.

New Zealand camp at Tel-el-Kebir where many of the Niueans served.
ROBERT HENRY FULTON COLLECTION, ALEXANDER TURNBULL LIBRARY, WELLINGTON, NEW ZEALAND, PA1-0-1841-01/1

CHAPTER 5

To Egypt

The weather was kinder on the voyage to Egypt than it had been on the trip to New Zealand, and the men were able to settle in to shipboard life without the constant problem of seasickness. They crossed the Tasman to the first port of call in Albany on the southwest coast of Australia, where the troops were confined to the ships while fresh supplies and fuel were loaded – the men were not allowed ashore because troops on previous ships had gone on drunken sprees and caused damage. The convoy then set out across the Indian Ocean towards Colombo. The tropical conditions on this leg of the voyage suited the Niueans, whereas the New Zealanders found the heat unbearable.

The ships called at Colombo for refuelling, and once again the men were denied shore leave because of the previous antics of Australian troops.[1] As the main city on the island of Ceylon (now Sri Lanka) – part of British India at the time – Colombo was an important experience for the Niuean soldiers, even though they were confined to the ship. It was the first time they had seen an Asian country, with its huge, bustling population. Vendors came out in small boats and jostled alongside the troopships, competing to sell food and novelty items, and the men were bombarded with new sights, sounds, languages, food and smells. Years later Tio still vividly recalled his 'visit to India'.[2]

The final leg of the voyage took the men across the Arabian Sea, past the port of Aden and into the Red Sea (Tahi Kula in Niuean). Their arrival in the Red Sea must have been a very emotional moment for the men from Niue: they were isolated and far from everything they knew, but here at last was a place of biblical significance that they had heard their pastors speak of back in the villages. Uea called to the men: 'come on deck to see for yourself the Red Sea you know from the Bible'.[3]

An outbreak of measles on board the troopship Navua *meant that when the vessel arrived in Suez on 15 March 1916 many of the Niueans were ill. 16/1062 Private Kaimanu of Hikutavake died on the day of arrival and now lies in the Suez War Memorial Cemetery.*
AUTHOR'S COLLECTION

This last leg was overshadowed by an outbreak of measles on board the *Navua*. By the time the ships reached their destination at the port of Suez at the northern limit of the Red Sea, several Niueans were seriously ill. The outbreak was not confined to Niueans but they suffered more severely because they had no immunity to diseases: when they contracted measles it often led to secondary infections that were even more life-threatening. By the time they docked at Suez the second Niuean casualty of the war had occurred: Private Kaimanu of Hikutavake died of 'pneumonia supervening measles' on board *Navua* on 15 March 1916, the day they arrived in Suez. He was taken from the ship and buried in the Protestant Cemetery in Suez.[4] Chaplain Uea was unable to conduct the burial service as he was among the 15 other Niueans suffering from measles who were transferred from the ship to the hospital in Suez. These men were kept in hospital for a week, then all except Private Pieti were transferred to a convalescent hospital in Cairo. Pieti was on the dangerously ill list and could not be moved: he remained alone in the hospital in Suez for nearly two months before he was shipped back to New Zealand on

SS *Maunganui*. The other men were either returned to the main body of Niueans when they were passed fit for duty, or were discharged back to New Zealand if they did not pass the medical test.[5]

Thus from the day of arrival in the Middle East the Niueans were separated from the main body as they were hospitalised. Some later returned to the Pioneers; others were left behind in hospitals and convalescent homes in Egypt and later France. Some were moved multiple times before they were shipped back to New Zealand. The effect of this on the men must have been particularly frightening because of their lack of English. While they were together as a group they could communicate among themselves in Vagahau Niue, and a few of them could pass on instructions to the others or at least give them some idea of what was happening. From their arrival in Suez, the process of separation began. Once the 140 men who had left New Zealand together disembarked from *Navua*, they were never again all together. Those who, like Pieti, found themselves totally alone in the strange environment of a foreign hospital must have felt especially displaced. The only comfort they could call on was their copy of the Niuean New Testament handed out in the church service back in Alofi. No wonder many Kiwi soldiers commented that the Niueans seemed a very religious people.

The main body of men who disembarked from the *Navua* were sent by train to the New Zealand base camp at Ismailia, north of Suez. The journey was their first opportunity to witness the landscape, sights and sounds of the country that was to be home for the next few weeks. A New Zealand soldier described the journey in his diary:

> For the first 20 or 30 miles [from Suez] nothing but desert on both sides … mud villages dot [the landscape] … Gradually the country became more fertile. The number of canals all flanked by date palm groves and other native trees, the camels and donkeys, the thousands of acres of maize … I could go on describing the fleeting sights we have of native life, the solitary mosque, the native cemeteries, the big, lazy Egyptian [astride] his miserable small donkey …[6]

On their arrival in Ismailia, the 3rd Maori Reinforcements were 'welcomed with ancient Maori ceremonial on the Egyptian desert'[7] and marched into camp. Then, because of the measles outbreak, they were put into isolation 400 metres west of the main camp. There they remained for seven days before being released and allotted to the various companies. The 3rd Reinforcements, which now consisted of 125 Niueans, 112 Māori and 45 Rarotongans, became part of the Pioneer Battalion, which had been formed on 20 February 1916 as the men were en route to Egypt. The Māori identity of this battalion was stamped on the regimental badge with a Māori warrior's face above a crossed pick and axe, flanked with fern leaves and with the words 'NZ Pioneers'. The pick and axe were symbolic of the work to be undertaken by the Pioneer Battalion: '[It] was not a fighting unit but a labour force trained and organised

The New Zealand General Hospital at Pont de Koubbeh in Cairo. Many Niueans were admitted to this hospital with bronchial and pulmonary infections, dysentery and enteritis. A New Zealand orderly commented that they were 'poor and difficult patients' as 'half of them couldn't speak English and they were terrified'.
NELSON PROVINCIAL MUSEUM COLLECTION, 300780

to work on engineering tasks, digging trenches, building roads, laying light railways, and the other hundred and one labouring jobs an army needs to do.'[8]

Once in the Pioneer Battalion, the Niueans were put through solid infantry training. This consisted of drilling, route marching, wagon loading, trench digging and rifle training, and it took place out in the desert in very hot and arduous conditions. During the last two weeks of March 1916 the weather in Egypt was described by one Australian soldier as 'very hot, very windy and unpleasant', 'still terrible … and last night it rained, very hard', 'another scorcher of a day', 'the heat today has been terrific and the flies a perfect pest', then, at the very end of March, 'the weather has suddenly cooled off again which means more sickness'.[9] This last diary entry is significant as it coincides with a lot more sickness in the Niuean ranks as they, too, succumbed to bronchial and pulmonary infections, dysentery and enteritis. These men were transferred to the New Zealand General Hospital at Pont de Koubbeh in Cairo, where they had to cope with a frightening and bewildering situation made worse by their illness. Colin Gordon, a New Zealand medical orderly working at Pont de Koubbeh when the Niueans arrived, described the process for admitting patients:

> patients were carried in on stretchers from the ambulances … laid on the floor each side of the corridor, one or two doctors checked the label attached giving a brief description of illness of each man … two orderlies then picked him up and delivered to the proper ward, after the orderly room clerk had taken his name, number, rank and unit for records. On arrival at the ward, Nurse in charge had a look at his label and according to the degree of disability directed the carriers to a bed … Those that still had on tunic and trousers were stripped at once, put into night shirt and the uniform was tied in a bundle labelled with number and name (boots, if any, were put in a bedside locker with paybook and personal possessions) and this bundle was taken … and lodged in the pack room.[10]

Gordon commented in particular on the Islanders in the hospital (he called them Cook Islanders, but this was the term commonly used for the Pacific Island men and he was in fact referring mainly to Niueans): 'They were terribly poor and difficult patients to deal with 'cause half of them couldn't

Egyptian children in Cairo watch the New Zealand troops. ROBERT HENRY FULTON COLLECTION, ALEXANDER TURNBULL LIBRARY, WELLINGTON, NEW ZEALAND PA1-O-1843-05/3

speak English and they were terrified of this dysentery.'[11] The difficulties were compounded by the fact that those with dysentery – a disease involving inflammation of the intestines – required a special diet but the orderlies were unable to explain this properly to the men. If mistakes were made with the food, the result was further diarrhoea, requiring a complete change of bedding and a washdown in Jeyes fluid.

Others suffered from the pulmonary complaints that were so prevalent among the Pacific Islanders. Private Ulukita was admitted to Pont de Koubbeh with pulmonary tuberculosis and was on the dangerously ill list for two weeks. Private Litioti was admitted to Pont de Koubbeh in early April, dangerously ill with pulmonary congestion; he recovered and was discharged to duty but was soon readmitted to the British Military Infectious Diseases Hospital at Choubra with dysentery. When he improved again he was transferred to the Aotea Convalescent Home at Heliopolis, a suburb of Cairo, and he remained there until he was invalided to New Zealand in late June, the only Niuean on the ship. By early April 1916, a full 52 per cent of the Niuean contingent had been or still were hospitalised. Some of these men recovered and were discharged to duty while others, like Ulukita and Litioti, were returned to New Zealand.

For those still in camp the daily routine was relieved by visits to Cairo: 25 per cent of the men at a time were given a pass until 10pm. The bustle and noise and smells of this large city were fascinating to all the New Zealand soldiers, including the Niueans. The red-light area of the city with its 'fale fifine', brothels, was the subject of much storytelling and boasting in later years – much of it probably pure fiction. The army authorities, in conjunction with the YMCA and the Salvation Army, worked hard to develop recreational facilities and events in the camps, and a new training depot was established northeast of Cairo at Tel-el-Kebir, 'right out in the desert and away from the temptations of the city'.[12] Some of the Niueans who were hospitalised were subsequently discharged back to duty there.

The troops received the occasional official visit, including from the Prince of Wales in late March. A Niuean soldier later recalled: 'The King's son visited us one day. The King's son met us and he was pleased to meet us, because Niue is not known by the world. He asked, "Where is Niue?"'[13] Days after this visit, the British Imperial Staff ordered the New Zealand Division to be moved to France to help on the Western Front. General Sir Archibald Murray, British commander-in-chief of the Mediterranean, visited the New Zealand troops accompanied by Lord Plunket, a former governor of New Zealand and chairman of the New Zealand War Contingent Association, based in London. Plunket later described the visit in a letter to the New Zealand minister of defence. Of the Pioneer Battalion, he said:

> [they] gave a farewell haka for the Commander-in-Chief … In addition to the Maori haka, the Rarotongans gave a dance and the Niue Islanders sang … The Battalion will be a very good one, and the Maoris and all the others in it seem to be very happy.[14]

The move to the Western Front was critical for the Niue contingent. Since their arrival in New Zealand for training, one of the difficulties was adjusting to climatic conditions they had never experienced before. The colder temperatures brought on bronchial and pulmonary conditions that they had no immunity to combat. For this reason the authorities in New Zealand had been concerned about sending the Niueans overseas. When the men were due to sail, the minister of defence, through the governor of New Zealand, had sent a request that the Niueans be stationed in a warm climate. The secretary of state for the colonies in London had replied, 'Army Council gladly agree to the inclusion in the Maori draft of Natives from Niue mentioned in your telegram of January 18th and will endeavour to utilise their services in a suitable climate.'[15] No promises were made, however, and when the order came to transfer the New Zealand Division to France the Niueans were included with the rest of the Pioneer Battalion. This action has been interpreted as a military blunder;[16] but Godley, the commander of the NZEF, made clear in a letter 10 days before the New Zealand troops were moved that he had considered the Niueans: 'The Niue Islanders and the Rarotongans seem alright and are going to France with the rest as at present arranged. The weather will be beginning to be warm by the time they arrive, so they should, I hope, be alright.'[17] The day before their departure from Egypt the Niuean men were given a medical examination and, of the original 140 who had sailed from New Zealand, 60 were found fit and able to continue on with the Pioneer Battalion.

It could be argued that the climate in Egypt was no kinder on the Niueans than spring in Europe – the desert climate was one of contrast between extremely high midday temperatures and freezing conditions at night. Eric Clarke of the Australian Imperial Force wrote that a sudden drop in temperature would result in sickness, and he often mentioned men suffering heatstroke or sunstroke. Route marches took place out in the desert and water supplies were soon exhausted. Thirst was made worse by the army reliance on bully beef or tinned corned beef, which is very salty and exacerbates thirst. Clarke spoke of having a violent headache and being feverish. In April he noted that on a route march he had got very hot. 'My mouth was parched and tongue and lips were swollen … When I did eventually get a drink it made me sick.'[18] This same condition was responsible for the second Niuean death in Egypt, after

16/1135 Private Tionemale of Hakupu was among the Niuean men who moved out from Egypt in early April as part of the newly formed Pioneer Battalion. He served on the Western Front until June, when the Niueans were moved out to England. Tionemale was in the second batch of Niueans sent back to New Zealand on the Arawa *in July 1916.*
COURTESY OF THE TIONEMALE FAMILY, NIUE

The climatic conditions in Egypt were difficult for all the troops. 16/1087 Private Mitikele of Hakupu died of heat stroke in Egypt. He is buried in the Tel-el-Kebir War Memorial Cemetery, one of only three men from the NZEF to lie there. AUTHOR'S COLLECTION

the first wave of troops had left for France. Private Mitikele of Hakupu had been admitted to the hospital at Pont de Koubbeh when the medical checks were done before the departure for France. Suffering from bronchitis, he had spent a month in hospital and was then discharged to duty at Tel-el-Kebir on 10 May 1916. Mitikele died of heatstroke on 16 May after doing sentry duty in the fierce midday sun. He was buried in the Tel-el-Kebir War Memorial Cemetery, one of only three New Zealand soldiers buried there. The climate in France proved difficult for the Niue men, but the sickness rates in Egypt suggest the results would have been little different if the men had stayed in the Middle East.

On 7 April 1916, 60 Niueans were part of the 976 members of the Pioneer Battalion who struck camp and left in two trainloads for Port Said on the Mediterranean coast. A New Zealander, travelling in the same convoy north, described the journey in his diary:

> at 6.30pm we moved out from camp with full swags up … rested for two hours, lying out in the desert under a brilliant sky and saying many times it was our last night in Egypt – not a man regrets leaving – A great long line

> of open trucks was our train, twenty men in each truck ... moved out at 11pm ... just as the day had been boiling hot, so the night was jolly cold, the wind whistling right over us as we lay stretched out ...[19]

At Port Said the Pioneer Battalion embarked on the transport ship *Canada* along with the Second Canterbury Battalion of Infantry. At 5am on 9 April *Canada* steamed out of the harbour bound across the Mediterranean for the French port of Marseilles. Usual danger-zone precautions were taken for the entire trip. A New Zealand soldier described the departure in his diary:

> Left Port Said ... with a fast gun-boat as escort. Passed a number of vessels including seven mine-sweepers. Strict orders to wear life belts all day and use them as pillows at night. Our course is a very zig-zag one, being altered about 70 degrees every quarter of an hour so as to lessen the chance of being torpedoed. Escort left us at dusk. Strict orders about showing no lights and [not] smoking on deck after dark.[20]

Canada carried enough boats to accommodate the nearly 2000 men on board although, as the official war history later pointed out, 'there would have been very small chance of launching them all in case of emergency'.[21] The men practised lifeboat drill en route. Lewis machine guns were mounted along each side of the ship and gun crews did four-hour reliefs by day and two hours by night. Fifty men at a time were on watch, looking for submarines: when they sighted one on the afternoon of 11 April the ship's course was altered and the steaming rate increased, and nothing more was seen of the raider. As the ship approached France, gas masks were issued, two to each man, and they practised gas drill. In spite of the precautions and constant state of alert, the journey was smooth and in some ways restful. 'The absolute rest and coolness of the sea is like a tonic. We sailed right up north of Crete today and we have the islands of the Grecian Archipelago on our port all day.'[22]

As the ships passed the coast of Sardinia the weather became colder, and when *Canada* arrived in Marseilles on 14 April 1916 there was a sea running and a cold wind blowing. All ships transporting the New Zealand Division made the journey safely across the Mediterranean. Now the troops prepared for a new theatre of war.

Corporal Tionesini of Hakupu, photographed before departure from Auckland.
COURTESY OF MRS MATILE F. TAUEVIHI, NIUE

CHAPTER 6

In France

In Marseilles there was a long wait when the ships arrived inside the breakwater then, after disembarkation, another long wait on the wharves for the trains that were to carry them north. One soldier noted, 'I suppose it is unfair to judge but Dunedin in mid-winter would be a welcome change – purely from a climatic viewpoint … several French Reservists assured me that it was an exceptional season.'[1]

The 60 Niuean soldiers in the Pioneer Battalion had had time to rest during the journey across the Mediterranean although, with nearly 2000 men on board, conditions were cramped and more men had fallen ill. Three of their number were taken to the No. 2 Australian General Hospital in Marseilles. This hospital had been set up in a chateau and, while officers were accommodated in the building, other ranks were housed in tents in the surrounding grounds. Private Kanatau of Makefu and Private Lauho of Lakepa were suffering from pleurisy and Private Paleko of Makefu had pneumonia. All were listed as seriously ill, and Kanatau and Paleko's condition deteriorated further, to dangerously ill. Lauho and Paleko recovered in time to rejoin the main body of Niueans as they were moved out to England in early June 1916, but Kanatau's experience was altogether more frightening.

From the moment of their arrival in southern France the Niueans were dealt with in a medical system that had been hastily created by the British authorities at the start of the war and, by 1916, had been streamlined and the recovery rate among troops greatly increased. The medical network channelled the injured and the ill through a system of clearing stations and hospitals that all eventually led to the channel ports on the northern coast of France and then on hospital ships to the south coast of England. From here men were transported to an increasingly complex network of hospitals and convalescent homes throughout the United Kingdom but especially in southern England, centred on London. Existing hospitals were expanded; other buildings were requisitioned and converted to hospitals; and private homes, especially large ones belonging to the upper classes, were redesigned as small hospitals and convalescent homes. Trucks were converted into ambulances; purpose-built ambulances were donated by families and groups; and railway carriages were converted into hospital wards on wheels. Mobile hospitals, including those operated by the New Zealand, Australian and Canadian army authorities, were set up but then moved as the troops moved. Most patients were housed in tents or huts – only officers received better accommodation. The Red Cross emblem clearly marked on all parts of this medical network was meant to keep the vehicles and buildings out of the conflict but this was not always honoured and there were many casualties.

Kanatau, Lauho and Paleko found themselves first in an Australian hospital that had been set up in Marseilles in anticipation of troops arriving from the Middle East. Kanatau was kept there from mid-April until early July. At that point, as the hospital was being prepared for a move to the north of France, he was transferred to Le Havre on the north coast of France. It is not recorded whether he was moved by ambulance truck or ambulance train but, given the distance, it was likely by train. He was then loaded into the British hospital ship *Laufranc*, taken across the channel and admitted to the Royal Victoria Hospital at Netley, Southampton. From there he was transferred to the No. 1 New Zealand General Hospital at Brockenhurst in Hampshire; here he was finally in the care of the medical authorities who were ultimately responsible for him, and after a month he was invalided back to New Zealand on the SS *Willochra* with one other Niuean, Lieutenant Corporal Talauta of Mutalau. Talauta had been admitted to hospital in Etaples in the north of France, dangerously ill with bronchitis. Transferred to England on the hospital ship *Brighton*, he had entered the 2nd London General Hospital at Chelsea and then the No. 2 New Zealand General Hospital at Walton-on-Thames before being finally discharged back to New Zealand. It must have been a lonely and bewildering journey.

Scene of French countryside taken from the troop train as men were transported north on a 58-hour journey to the combat zone of the Western Front. ROBERT HENRY FULTON COLLECTION, ALEXANDER TURNBULL LIBRARY, WELLINGTON, NEW ZEALAND, PA1-O-1841-11/4

The main group of Niueans in Marseilles were now part of the great mass of New Zealand soldiers who were trained north in a 58-hour journey that official reports described in terms of the beautiful spring countryside but that the men wrote about, in their private diaries, in terms of the cramped conditions and the outbreak of disease. The Niueans, when they caught glimpses of the French countryside outside, would have noted the new scenery. The official history recorded:

> at the outset the tedium was relieved by the exquisite scenery of the Rhone Valley. The fresh green of the trees and rich grasses, the early flowers in the meadows, and the sunny woodlands, tricked out with the blossoms and pageantry of Spring, were in striking contrast with the monotony of the parched desert. The troops were in highest spirits. With lively curiosity they eyed the riverside mansions and trim villages, and exchanged pleasantries with the fishermen on the banks and the cheering girls at the stations.[2]

The soldiers, though, commented that the trains were very crowded with little chance of a comfortable rest for anyone on the journey, and that there was 'a terrible lot of diarrhoea and sickness on the train'.[3]

The journey took them through Versailles on the outskirts of Paris then to the north. 'Thereafter the grey rain-sodden skies, bleak country and bitter winds of the north formed a more appropriate setting for the grim business that lay in front.'[4] At the railhead at Steenbeque in the north, not far from the Western Front, the men detrained and continued on foot to Morbeque where the Pioneers took up billets in the local school and in three farms within a two-mile (3km) radius of the village square. The billets needed to be cleaned before the men could settle in, but almost immediately they were ordered to move on to Sercus and install themselves once more. After the journey from Egypt, this was the first march for the soldiers and it was on the hard metalled roads of France, quite different from the desert sands. The Niueans found the whole march difficult, especially as the weather was very cold and miserable with frequent rain. The medical officer for the Pioneers reported to headquarters on the state of the Niue Islanders:

> On the termination of the railway journey from Marseilles these men were absolutely exhausted and, with the exception of one or two, needed assistance in carrying their ordinary equipment … Sixteen Niueans required immediate evacuation into the No. 1 New Zealand Field Ambulance. These were the worst cases.[5]

Unlike the huge tent cities of the camps in Egypt, in the north of France the soldiers were housed in buildings. One soldier explained the arrangement:

> Our billets are in barns … we do our own cooking with our own rations and the inhabitants of the village are paid so much for providing sleeping accommodation … We found that there were no facilities for cooking at all [when we arrived] … it was raining and had been for several days.[6]

Official reports confirmed difficult climatic conditions which necessitated the issue of a second blanket, turned all gun parks and horse lines into quagmires and prevented training.

The northern plains of France are known for their bleak desolation and the cold, foggy weather that rolls in from the North Sea. The landscape consisted of unfenced fields cultivated by women and old men, since the younger men had left to serve in the French army. Small agricultural villages dotted the farmland. Each village was marked by its tall church spire, perhaps a town wall, red-brick houses, and a large tree-shaded chateau on the outskirts of town. From a high point it was possible to look out over the plains and see the slag heaps and pit heads that marked this part of France as a major coal-producing region. Towards the east, dull, far-off rumbles were often heard and in the evening 'the rockets and flares of the trenches described slow parabolas on the screen of the dark heavens'.[7]

Despite the weather, the troops organised their billets and settled in to their new environment. The Pioneers were kept busy with route marches, bayonet fighting practice, gas mask practice and platoon drill. Two strongpoints on the road southwest of Sercus were completed and bridgehead work was undertaken over the nearby River Lys. Part of the Pioneer Battalion was also employed in a tree-felling programme; the logs were to be milled for construction work in the trenches and along the roads. On the medical side, the inoculation of all troops for para-typhoid was completed. A battalion church parade was held in the village square in Sercus on Good Friday, 21 April 1916, and there were regular church services on Sundays.

During their time in Sercus three more Niueans were hospitalised and then transferred on through the medical chain to England. Corporal Manatoa of Tuapa, Private Pakitau of Mutalau and Corporal Hipa of Hikutavake all became ill in late April and were admitted to field hospitals and subsequently transferred by hospital train then hospital ship to England. Manatoa and Pakitau were both admitted to the 2nd London General Hospital, but Hipa spent time alone at the Royal Victoria Hospital at Netley. All three were eventually discharged to join the main Niuean group gathered at Hornchurch.

The next move came on 1 May when the Pioneers were shifted closer to the front with a 17-mile (27km) march to Estaires. A diary entry describes the march:

> Monday 1 May … reveille at 4am. Marched off at 6 … Men were dropping out on the roadside before the ten mile mark was reached … stopped for

> midday meal … even tucker was neglected until we had bathed [our feet] in the ditches at the side of the road. All through the afternoon men continued to fall out. We passed hundreds. The motor ambulances were running continuously throughout the day picking up men and carrying them on.[8]

In spite of the difficulty of the march the medical records show no Niuean casualties for that day, and once the men were installed in their new billets in Estaires most of those who had been hospitalised on arrival in the north rejoined the group. The exceptions were Private Falaoa of Avatele, Corporal Talauta of Mutalau and Private Tionemouga of Liku who were all sent by hospital ship to England. They all eventually rejoined the Niuean group at Hornchurch but not before hospital stays in London and, for Tionemouga, in Birmingham.

New Zealand troops march on the road to Armentières. Truck convoys move past them and some men pull wagon-loads of equipment. The Niueans were part of the group being moved into the combat zone to work as labourers in the Pioneer Battalion.

NATIONAL ARMY MUSEUM, NEW ZEALAND, 2007-549

At Estaires training and preparations continued – it was only a matter of time until the Pioneer Battalion was to be moved to the front to relieve British Pioneers. From Estaires they could hear the noise from the front – 'we could see in the distance the flashes and the noise and the thunder of the guns';[9] and for the first time they saw a new weapon of war – the plane. German planes flew over the area regularly: they were an important method of observation and could spot troop concentrations, note the condition of trenches and the position of wires and dugout entrances. From 300m a pilot could distinguish between British and German troops, especially because of the round tin helmet worn by the British and New Zealand troops. On 8 May a German plane dropped a large bomb 55m from one group of Pioneers; although no one was injured, it left a large crater in the ground – and a considerable impression on the minds of the men.

The order to move again, this time to Armentières and into the combat zone, came on 15 May:

> All hands on fatigue cleaning up all morning. In afternoon Battalion all had hot baths and got clean clothes ... Battalion left Estaires in full marching order ... at 7.45pm (for a march of about 11 miles)[18km]. Battalion had usual hourly halts and an uneventful march – no one fell out and all marched well. Arrived Armentières 12.30am and billeted in cotton factory of Charvel Frères, rue de Bizet, just north of town of Armentières on River Lys.[10]

The land on the opposite bank of the River Lys was enemy territory, farmland that had been abandoned by the owners in the face of the German advance. Farm implements lay rusting where they had been dropped and the whole area was criss-crossed with wire entanglements and seamed with German trenches.

In Armentières approximately one third of the prewar civilian population of 20,000 remained. They ran all kind of shops, restaurants and estaminets – small cafés, often in home kitchens, where food and drink could be purchased. A private in the Wellington Infantry Company described one such estaminet, just outside Armentières:

Communication trench near Armentières. Trenching work involved digging and sandbagging, transporting timber frames and corrugated iron for support of the walls and laying duckboards to walk on. Because it was an active combat zone, much of the work was done at night. NATIONAL ARMY MUSEUM NEW ZEALAND, 2007-183

> At Bac St Maur there was a woman we knew as Marie. I don't know what her other name was; she was a thin, worried woman about thirty five, forty. Her husband was in the French Army and she would sell us eggs and chips or anything at all … we'd be all crowded round in her kitchen round the big stove. And she'd be selling us wine and that sort of thing and … if anyone had raised a hand or said anything wrong to that woman, he'd have been given a thrashing and dumped outside.
>
> Well in that kitchen of hers there was a hole right through the corner where a five-nine shell had gone through, taken the corner off, and it was packed up with sandbags and she was still carrying on.[11]

Work now began in the trenches and on the communications about town. It was considered unsafe to move parties into and out of the trenches during daylight, so the work was done at night. The low-lying, waterlogged plains of northern France made trench digging tedious and physically demanding, and the amount of artillery fire made work dangerous, even at night. A sentry system with machine-gun positions was maintained and each trench line was guarded by extensive wire entanglements. The men could approach the front-line trenches by means of connecting communication trenches. If these were under fire they could use overland routes marked by pegs painted white on the side turned from the enemy, to facilitate movement at night. Trenching activity involved digging and sandbagging, transporting timber frames in for support and placing duckboards at the bottom. The work was carried out in the midst of mud, cold – and rats. Having set out for work at 7.30pm the men would return around 3.30am, moving in small parties in case of attack. They would sleep during the morning and then assemble in the afternoon for gas drill, rifle inspection and marching.[12]

In the last week of May the Pioneers suffered a growing number of casualties. The first combat casualties from artillery fire occurred among the working parties at the frontline, and heavy shelling of Armentières with high explosives led to casualties among men on leave in the town. By now two more Niueans were seriously ill. Corporal Tionesini of Hakupu was admitted to the British No. 8 Casualty Clearing Station in Bailleul with pneumonia and died three days later, on 31 May 1916. And on that day Private Tauetuli of Liku was

Sunset over tents at the NZ Reinforcement Camp at Etaples in the northwest of France. The Nlueans on the Western Front were moved here at the end of May 1916, and were joined by a second group who had just arrived from Egypt.
ALEXANDER TURNBULL LIBRARY, WELLINGTON, NEW ZEALAND, 1/2-013018-G

Private Taveli of Avatele. Taveli served in Egypt and France before being sent with the main body of Niueans to Hornchurch. He returned to New Zealand on the Arawa. *He was one of a small percentage of Niuean servicemen who were not hospitalised while on overseas service.*
COURTESY OF AOKUSO PAVIHI, AVATELE

admitted to the 1st Canadian Clearing Station with pneumonia after exposure while on duty; he was one of 134 patients admitted that day – a big increase in the daily rate from earlier in the month. Tauetuli died on 9 June 1916 and was buried in the Bailleul Communal Cemetery along with Tionisini. There was fighting in Bailleul throughout the war: nearly 4500 soldiers now lie buried there, including 252 from the NZEF.

In late May the authorities decided to withdraw the Niuean troops from the Western Front and send them to England for rest and recuperation before returning them to New Zealand. This decision evoked strong words between Allen and Godley. Allen was annoyed when he learnt of the withdrawal of the Niuean men and Godley, after first being very vague about what was happening, later claimed it was a decision he disagreed with, but it was made during his absence.[13] The order certainly came from the headquarters of the New Zealand Division and read:

> it has now been decided to collect all Niue Islanders with the N.Z.E.F. and return them to N.Z. You will please take steps to forward all Niue Islanders now with the [Pioneer] Battalion to the base, Etaples, for passage to England. They should be sent in one party, under proper conduct, with rolls and other papers complete.[14]

It appears that the plight of the Niueans had been discussed at the New Zealand Division headquarters – in particular the medical reports that showed the high number of cases of pneumonia. Of the men who had remained in Egypt when the division was transferred to France in early April 1916, some had subsequently been sent back to New Zealand as medically unfit, but 52 of the men had returned to duty and, on 20 May, had embarked on the transport ship *Ivernia* at Alexandria for passage to Marseilles. The army had to decide where to deploy these men once they arrived in France. Sending them to the front would be sure to result in further illness, so on 25 May, as the second group was landing in Marseilles, the order was given to gather all the Niueans together in Etaples for passage to England. This was a humane decision. There was more illness and more deaths on the journey to England and home; only 18 per cent of the original group of Niuean recruits completed their service without being hospitalised. World War I was an unimaginable waste of human life, but fortunately, in the case of the Niueans, a sensible decision was made before it was too late.

The process of reuniting the Niuean soldiers now began. When *Ivernia* berthed in Marseilles the Niuean group on board was trained directly to Etaples in the north of France. They reached the New Zealand base camp on 28 May. The group at Armentières was marched out under the command of Second Lieutenant George Fromm on 30 May and, on 1 June 1916, a wonderful reunion took place at Etaples. The men had been isolated, when on duty or in hospital, by their lack of English: they must have revelled in the presence of their friends and countrymen again. The camp at Etaples was enormous, with up to 25,000 men at any one time, but in those first days of June there was a small corner of the camp that was Niuean.

On 5 June 1916 they crossed the Channel and arrived for the first time in 'the Great Britain ruled by King George V'.[15] A number of men were still in hospital in Egypt and France; some had already been transported to England by hospital ship; others had been shipped back to New Zealand, medically unfit for active service. And the route these men had followed through Egypt and France was marked by four Niuean headstones lying among the graves of men and women from all parts of the British Empire.

Entrance to Grey Towers, Hornchurch, England. The hospitalisation rate among the Niueans was so high that they were withdrawn from the Western Front at the end of May 1916 and sent to the New Zealand Convalescent Hospital at Hornchurch.
ALEXANDER TURNBULL LIBRARY, WELLINGTON, NEW ZEALAND, 1/2-013942-G

CHAPTER 7

Hornchurch, England

When the New Zealand Division was moved from Egypt to France, a base depot had to be set up in England. The site chosen was in Hornchurch – a village with tree-shaded lanes in the county of Essex, 32 kilometres east of London, surrounded by farms and market gardens. The owners of Grey Towers, a large country house in the village, had recently died and the building was available. Accommodation huts were built beneath the trees in the magnificent park, clustering around the ancient, ivy-clad manor house. This is where the Niuean troops were sent from Etaples – just as the base depot at Hornchurch was being converted to the main New Zealand convalescent hospital in England.[1]

The arrival of 102 Niuean soldiers on 5 June 1916 must have created an impression on the local people. The men were weary and, in many cases, debilitated from illness: many of them spent time in hospital in Hornchurch and some were so ill they had to be transferred to other hospitals. From reports of the time – particularly the diary of St Andrew's Church in Hornchurch – it is clear the people of this small village took these Niuean men to their hearts. They referred to Niue as 'in the South Sea Islands',[2] conjuring visions of tropical, sun-drenched, palm-clad islands far away from the madness that was Europe.

The church diary noted that these men lived entirely on fruit in their own country, so Reverend A.J. Parry, assistant pastor, arranged for a daily collection of bananas and other fruit for them from the people of the village. Parry conducted a service each morning in the hospital and the diary records that this service was translated by a 'native catechist' – presumably Sergeant Uea. He had come through with the second group of men from Egypt in late May

Hospital grounds, Hornchurch. Barracks were built in the grounds of Grey Towers, and paths and gardens were laid out. Here men recovered sufficiently to be either sent back to France or shipped home to New Zealand.
ALEXANDER TURNBULL LIBRARY, WELLINGTON, NEW ZEALAND, 1/2-013954-G

and was with the large group that arrived in Hornchurch in early June. Uea was in the first group of men to be transferred back to New Zealand on 17 June 1916, and it is unclear what happened to the church services after that. People went out of their way to be kind to the men from Niue: they recognised that the isolation and homesickness they must be feeling was made worse by their lack of English.

Caring for New Zealand troops in hospital or convalescent homes in England was something that had been thought about and planned for from the start of the war. In the very first month of the conflict Sir Thomas MacKenzie, New Zealand high commissioner in London, had chaired a meeting to set up an organisation whose aim was to 'afford assistance to and extra comforts for the members of the New Zealand Contingents while in this country and abroad'.[3] The New Zealand War Contingent Association (NZWCA) consisted of people in the United Kingdom who were New Zealanders or had a close association with the country. They were involved in setting up the first New Zealand hospital in Britain at Walton-on-Thames. Much of their work involved visiting men invalided to Britain from the Dardanelles in 1915 and, from 1916 until the war ended, from the Western Front. New Zealand Military Headquarters sent the names and hospital details of sick and wounded soldiers to the NZWCA in London. The visiting committee would arrange for an official visitor to call on each man, and they would make up parcels with supplies for the patient. Hospital visitors reported back to head office with updates on patients, their progress and requirements. An entertainment committee organised concerts and outings for men convalescing, and they set up clubs in all the New Zealand hospitals and convalescent homes, including Hornchurch, to provide friendly, familiar surroundings where men could gather for a cup of tea and a chat. 'We run them on thoroughly New Zealand lines – New Zealand ladies in charge, New Zealand cooking, New Zealand papers and periodicals on the tables and the whole organisation of the association behind them.'[4]

The first big influx of New Zealand men to hospitals in Britain came with the Gallipoli campaign in 1915. As the NZWCA swung into operation they discovered that some of the wounded were Māori, so they found a visitor who could speak fluent Māori – Sybil Lee, who had worked as a missionary with the Church Missionary Society (CMS) at Tokomaru Bay on the East Coast of the North Island for many years. She had contracted typhoid fever there and was ill for some time; she had returned to London on furlough for rest, and was there when the war broke out. Sybil asked permission to remain in England 'so that she might minister to the Maori sick and wounded',[5] and she became an active member of the NZWCA. By late 1915 she had been designated 'official Maori visitor'.

By 1916 the NZWCA had nearly 175 official visitors working among the 'blue boys' – a reference to the blue uniform items worn by men who were convalescing. Sybil was kept extremely busy: she spent the morning at the

New Zealand workrooms, 'where we have a stupendous amount of sewing on hand'[6] making bed linen, pyjamas and shirts for the growing numbers of men arriving from France. In the afternoon she visited the Māori soldiers who were 'spread out over so many hospitals. Some of the very Maori ones are lonely.'[7] By 'very Maori' she was referring to those who spoke little or no English. Sybil soon realised there were a small number of Niuean men arriving who were in a similar situation, so she set about finding someone who could converse with them in their own language. It is likely she used her missionary society connections to make a link between Niue and the London Missionary Society, who knew the exact person to help her – a woman who was fluent in Vagahau Niue, having spent over 40 years on the island and now retired and living in London, moreover a woman loved and respected by the Niueans: Sarah Lawes.

Frank and Sarah Lawes had gone to Niue in 1868 after Frank had completed training in England at an LMS institution. His older brother, Reverend George Lawes, and his wife Fanny had been working on the island since 1861 – the first Pālagi to live there. After four years of working with his brother, George was sent to open the LMS mission in Port Moresby and Frank took charge of the Niue mission. Frank and Sarah remained in this post for 42 years; nine of their 10 children were born on the island, and one was buried there. They were fluent in Vagahau Niue, they cared about the people and they came to be much loved and respected. When they retired they settled in West Ealing in London, but they kept in regular contact by mail with friends and colleagues back in the Pacific. When Sybil wrote to Sarah in May 1916 to ask if she could help by visiting the Niueans in London hospitals, Sarah agreed – even though Frank was unwell and she herself was now elderly and somewhat infirm.[8]

Sarah's first hospital visit was to the 2nd London General Hospital in Chelsea in May 1916. Here a college and school had been commandeered to create a hospital that could accommodate over 1000 patients. It was close to Chelsea Station, and a wall on one side of the site was demolished so that patients could be brought by ambulance train directly to the station and into the hospital. Sarah received a letter telling her about a Niuean in this hospital who was 'very lonely as he could not speak English so the next day I went to

Sarah Lawes, wife of the missionary Reverend Frank Lawes, photographed in London c. 1903. Standing at rear is Farani, Frank, the youngest of the Lawes children. The three young ones are Sarah and Frank's grandchildren. In 1916 they served afternoon tea to the Niuean group who enjoyed a tour of London with Sarah.
COURTESY OF LAWES FAMILY, LONDON

16/1044 Private Falaoa of Avatele. A young man isolated and bewildered in a London hospital, he was overjoyed to receive a visit from an elderly Englishwoman, Sarah Lawes, who knew his family and village well. She explained what he needed to know in his own language and possibly helped Falaoa to recover sufficiently to return home.
COURTESY OF MELE VEKULA-MOONEN, WELLINGTON

him and found his name was Falaoa, Tosene's son at Avatele; he was quite well save for "trench foot" and they could not make him understand that he must be very careful or he would lose his feet, so I told him.'[9]

Trench foot was a fungal infection caused by prolonged exposure of the feet to damp, unsanitary and cold conditions; it was especially common in the trenches of World War I, hence the name. If not treated it usually resulted in gangrene, and amputation was the only remedy. The military authorities did everything they could to combat this condition, including regular foot inspections, application of whale oil to help waterproof the feet, a change of socks twice a day and regular washing of socks. These measures were helpful when men were resting behind the lines, but they were impossible to enforce when men were digging or fighting in the trenches.

What a joyful reunion took place when Sarah Lawes went to visit Falaoa: not only did she speak Vagahau Niue, she knew his village and his parents and family very well. His father, Tosene, was what was known as a 'native pastor'. He and his wife had lived at the LMS training college in Alofi, and while Tosene studied scripture with Frank Lawes, his wife had learnt sewing and English and arithmetic with Sarah. They had then gone out to serve at the LMS church in Avatele. The native pastors ran the local church and the school attached to it. They were respected in the village because of their church links and their ability to read and write English. It might seem strange that Falaoa was not able to speak English, but he was the son chosen to be taught the traditional Niuean skills of bushcraft and fishing. His brother Fasene was taught English and had been working as a pupil teacher in the school at Avatele. He, too, was in the Niue contingent and, because of his skill in English, was given the rank of corporal and used as an interpreter at Narrow Neck and in Egypt. He had become ill in Egypt and was invalided home, so Falaoa was very much alone until he was reunited with Sarah Lawes.[10]

Sarah also visited three men in the No. 1 New Zealand Hospital at Walton-on-Thames, west of London: Manatoa, Pakitau and Talauta were convalescing there after their ordeals in France. Once more there was a joyful reunion between young men from a distant Pacific island and an elderly Englishwoman.

Mele, a great-granddaughter of Falaoa, meets up with Frances, a great-granddaughter of Sarah Lawes in Wellington, New Zealand, in December 2016 – 100 years after the retired missionary wife visited the young Niuean soldier in a London hospital.
COURTESY OF ANNA COTTRELL, WELLINGTON

The biggest reunion, however, was at Hornchurch where just over 100 Niuean men were recuperating. Frank and Sarah Lawes had an idea this group was arriving in England. As Sarah later wrote to James Cullen:

> First I had a letter from Uea dated Cairo and I sent him a long letter; then I heard from our son Alfred that he had met Uea and Kamupeli as they were stationed near to him in France!! After writing again to Uea we had another letter from him saying they were at Hornchurch in Essex, the camp where Alfred and Farani [the Lawes' son Frank] were when they first joined, so on Whit Sunday Mr Lawes and I, Maggie and Neville went to see them. The first we saw there was Falaile (Mutalau) who used to be servant with us when a boy; they were very pleased to see us and Mr Lawes talked more Niuean than I had heard for a very long time.[11]

The reunion was reported in an LMS publication: 'Mr and Mrs Lawes were asked to go to [the Niueans at Hornchurch], being the only English people who knew the language! Great was the delight of people and missionaries to thus meet again.'[12] The Niuean men believed that Reverend Lawes had had some influence in persuading the military authorities to withdraw the Niueans from the Western Front. No documented evidence has been found to support this, however; and of the two, Sarah was much more active in following the Niueans' movements than Frank.

Sarah Lawes, following the example of the NZWCA, organised for a group of Niueans to visit London: the idea was that one man from each village would go there with Uea. But the very week the trip was to take place, the first group of 40 men, including Uea, were marched out of Hornchurch for shipping back to New Zealand. Nevertheless, 10 of the remaining men took the train to London: Sarah met them at Victoria Station and they were taken on a tour of the city:

> We had dinner at a place opposite [the station] and then we went to the Houses of Parliament, saw both houses and then to Westminster Abbey, saw Livingstone's grave; from there to St Paul's Cathedral, saw the grave of Gordon on which wreaths were placed for Kitchener; from there we went to the Tower, saw the Crown Jewels and the Armoury, they were very interested in the latter and can understand better Eph VI[13]... then we went to Buckingham Palace and saw the memorial to Queen Victoria.[14]

It was a tour laced with imperial and LMS overtones. David Livingstone, the British doctor and explorer, had worked in Africa for the LMS, opening up the vast unexplored centre of the continent to missionaries. He was a hero to members of the LMS, and the Lawes no doubt had taught and preached about him on Niue. Charles Gordon and Horatio Kitchener were both associated with the British conquest of Egypt and the Sudan. At the outbreak of World War I Kitchener was secretary of state for war; he drowned in 1916, shortly before the Niueans visited Gordon's tomb (wreaths were left here for Kitchener because of the link to Gordon and the fact that Kitchener had no known grave). The visit to Buckingham Palace and the Queen Victoria memorial was a must for Pacific Islanders who had grown up in awe of the queen:

> The oldest native in the South Seas remembers no sovereign's name but hers. She was a real person to them all; a lady who had made them her especial care, had sent the gospel to them, and had bade them lay aside their clubs, and

LEFT: *Headstone of Vasau and Moki.* RIGHT: *Headstone of Filitoua and Taleva. All four Niuean men died of pneumonia during their stay at Hornchurch and are buried in the churchyard of St Andrew's. These are official headstones but, unusually, there are two names to each one. The presence of these men in Hornchurch has resulted in close bonds between the English village and the tiny Pacific island.* AUTHOR'S COLLECTION

> live in peace, order and equity. Vika, as they called her affectionately – Vika, after whom they named their girl-children – was the benign, all-powerful chief, whose house was built upon the coral strand of Lonitoni (London). She read their letters, with her own eyes, and had her captains sit before her on the floor-mats while she gave them messages for the brown folk in the far islands.[15]

The day was rounded off with a visit to the home of Alfred Lawes, the oldest of the Lawes children. He was serving in France but the men were entertained by 'Mrs Alfred' and served 'a good tea' by Alfred's three children.

When Sarah Lawes realised that, of the group, five were from Alofi, she requested that another group be sent from Hornchurch with representatives from other villages. Seven others were given a similar tour, although there were no representatives from Fatiau or Avatele. There is no doubt that the tour of London was a highlight for those who were able to participate, and Sarah Lawes had it in mind that all the villages would hear about the sights from their representatives.

John Arundel, a supporter of the LMS and friend of the Lawes who had developed guano and copra interests in the Pacific in the latter part of the nineteenth century and had drawn much of his labour force from Niue, sent money to get 'comforts' for the men. Sarah decided that,

> instead of buying tobacco I would buy a pencil each for their wives or matua [elders], as a souvenir of their visit to England and I got 150 at greatly reduced rate 3/- a dozen and I am sending them to [Rev. Cullen] either to keep till the men return or distribute beforehand whichever you think best. I hope Mr Cornwall will not charge duty on them.[16]

While the men who were well or recovering at Hornchurch were enjoying the pleasant surroundings at Grey Towers and perhaps an outing with Mrs Lawes in London, others were being admitted to the camp hospital. A number of deaths occurred there that cemented ties between Hornchurch and Niue. Soon after he arrived from France, Private Vasau of Alofi was hospitalised with pneumonia and placed on the dangerously ill list; he died in the depot hospital on 11 June 1916 and was buried two days later, after a service in St Andrew's: the church diary records the burial of 'Private Vasau, a Christian soldier from Niue Island, one of the South Sea Islands, attached to the New Zealand Contingent'.[17] The diary also notes that the Niue Islanders had been converted to Christianity by missionaries of the Congregational Church, and so a Congregational minister was brought in to conduct the service at St Andrew's. The same minister, Reverend J. Benson Evans, was back in the church the following day to conduct the service for Private Taleva of Tamakautoga who had died of pneumonia, also at the depot hospital.

While the burials were taking place for Vasau and Taleva, three other Niueans were on the dangerously ill list in the Hornchurch camp hospital. Private Lavaika of Alofi and his brother Private Finiki and Private Filitoua of Makefu would have been unaware of the departure on 17 June of the first

Interior of St Andrew's Church, Hornchurch, where four funeral services were conducted for Niueans in June and July 1916. One local historian described 'the sun filtering through the south windows onto the coffin and the church crowded with … fellow soldiers'.
AUTHOR'S COLLECTION FROM A PHOTO GIFTED BY TERRY TRIMMER, UPMINSTER, UK, FOR 'MY HEART IS CRYING A LITTLE'

group of 40 men returning to New Zealand. Filitoua died two days later, and Reverend Evans was called in yet again to conduct a burial service for a Niuean. The two brothers from Alofi remained on the dangerously ill list, and now another Niuean, Private Moki, from the village of Fatiau, joined them in hospital. Moki died of pneumonia on 30 June and was the fourth and final Niuean to be buried in the St Andrew's churchyard. The entry in the church diary is of special significance:

> July 3 [1916] – Burial of His Highness the Prince Rangitira (known as Prince Moki), Private 16/1088, New Zealand Expeditionary Force, Base Depot. Prince Moki, who was 21 years of age, was a son of the ruling chief of the Island of Niue. He had seen active service in Egypt and on the Western Front. He died of pneumonia at Grey Towers Camp ...[18]

Whatever stories Moki told, he has certainly won himself a special place in Hornchurch history– although he was not related to Togia, the patuiki or ruling chief of Niue. Moki was the only representative from the tiny village of Fatiau on the south coast of the island. Togia was from the village of Tuapa and had no sons serving in the Niue contingent. Furthermore, the office of patuiki was not a hereditary one and the title would not have been passed on to a son. Moki, however, not only gained himself the English title His Highness but also the Māori title Rangatira, chief. It would appear that he was something of a character and the other men obviously liked him, as they were happy to be part of this fraud. Some say that Moki's only real claim to fame was that he was the owner of the largest pair of feet in the whole contingent and had needed boots made especially for him. Perhaps the joke about being son of the 'king' was a reflection of the north–south rivalry that was often evident on Niue: Moki was from the south and Togia from the north; or maybe it had something to do with the generally low esteem in which Togia was held by his fellow countrymen.[19] Whatever the reason, the idea of 'a Polynesian Prince buried in our churchyard'[20] captured the imagination of the people of Hornchurch. One local history records the event:

> St Andrew's would have seen many moving and unusual sights in its long history but the funeral of Prince Rangitira must have ranked high on the

> list. The sun filtering through the south windows on to the coffin and the church crowded with his fellow soldiers. The villagers, many of them already dressed in black to mourn their own dead, came to pay their last respects to a man they had come to know and like. The service ended with the Prince's comrades singing a funeral hymn in their native language to a native tune.[21]

The people of Hornchurch will hopefully forgive the pranks of these men who led them astray as to the real identity of Moki. He lies now in their churchyard, where he shares a headstone with Vasau. Behind is the headstone shared by Filitoua and Taleva. These two memorials represent a tangible link between the people of an English village and the people of a far distant Pacific island.

Moki was the last of the Niueans to die in Hornchurch; but men stayed in the village for several months to come. After the main groups of men had left, individual Niueans continued to arrive from hospitals elsewhere in England to convalesce and await shipment back to New Zealand. The Lawes did not visit Hornchurch again – although it was not the end of hospital visiting for Sarah.

The brothers Lavaika and Finiki were moved from Hornchurch in early July to convalesce in a small hospital in Belgravia, a very exclusive and fashionable suburb of London. As happened frequently during the war because upper-class women wanted to help the war effort in some way, a house on Eaton Square had been purchased and equipped by the Countess of Dundonald to provide 60 beds for military convalescence. It opened in 1916, under the management of the Hon. Margaret Amherst and staffed by members of the Norfolk Voluntary Aid Detachment (VAD), who had obtained permission to transfer to the London area. From the outbreak of war, Margaret Amherst had worked in fundraising for the war effort and in public speaking to encourage people to train for voluntary ambulance work. Now in charge of Lady Dundonald's hospital, she was very interested in the two 'South Sea islanders' who arrived in her care. She read Basil Thomson's account of his voyage to Niue in 1900,[22] and she was very pleased when the NZWCA arranged for Sarah Lawes to visit these two young men.

The experience must have been memorable for Lavaika and Finiki. From a large military camp and hospital, they now found themselves in an exclusive home in a tranquil part of London being cared for by a woman who hailed from the upper echelons of English society. She was obviously as moved by the experience as they were:

> Two [Niueans] came to the hospital of which I am in charge, where they quickly became general favourites. They were cheerful and patient and obliging. As soon as they were able to do so they helped the nurses in the cleaning of the wards and the work of the pantry; and were most capable in their work. They did not care much for games, and despised 'fancy work', but spent their time in writing and reading the Bible, about the only book printed in their language. Their greatest pleasure was a visit from Mrs Lawes, who kindly came very often to chat with them in their own language. Their faces would light up with joy when 'Misi Farani Fifine' ... was announced, and through her we were able to find out anything they wanted to have or to know.[23]

Sarah took the two young men on one of her London tours of the main sights such as St Paul's and Westminster Abbey, as well as the big department stores. Amherst also noted that 'they visited the zoo, and were amazed at the great animals, as there are no wild beasts on Niue, and Madame Tussaud's impressed them greatly'. When the two Niueans left England on the New Zealand hospital ship *Marama* on 31 August 1916, Amherst reflected:

> We shall always think fondly of Finiki and Lavaika, they will have ever a warm corner in our hearts, and now we miss them sadly for they are on their way home in a hospital ship bound for New Zealand. We wonder what they will tell their friends about their experiences, what will have struck them most. We trust they will think well of us, but what a strange impression they will have of western civilisation![24]

These comments could have applied to any of the Niueans who had spent time in England. And now they were returning home, back to the island of Niue. What thoughts and impressions of Western civilisation did they take with them?

SERGEANT PULU,
of Niue Island,
Died of wounds.

PRIVATE PENI,
of Niue Island,
Died of wounds.

PRIVATE FILITONA,
of Niue Island,
Died of pneumonia.

CORPORAL HIPA,
of Niue Island,
Wounded.

PRIVATE TINEATAMA,
of Niue Island,
Died of sickness.

PRIVATE PINEKI,
of Niue Island,
Died of sickness.

The Auckland Weekly News *regularly published head-and-shoulder photos of casualties during the war. The newspaper relied on families to send in these photos. The only time Niuean men appear in these pages was October 1916 after most of the men had returned to New Zealand. The Niueans are Filitoua, who died at Hornchurch; Peni, Pulu, Tiueatama and Pineki, who were buried at sea during the voyage of the* Corinthic; *and Hipa, who returned on the hospital ship* Marama. SIR GEORGE GREY SPECIAL COLLECTIONS, AUCKLAND LIBRARIES, NEW ZEALAND, AWNS-19161005-40-17

CHAPTER 8

The return home

The Niuean soldiers made the journey back to New Zealand in nine different troopships.[1] Those who had been hospitalised in Egypt and then pronounced unfit for further service were returned from Suez. The first group made the return journey in May 1916, following the same route by which they had come to the Middle East; and the rest returned in *Ulimaroa* in June.

The first large group of Niueans to return to New Zealand from England left Southampton on the *Corinthic* on 17 June 1916. This group consisted of 40 men who were identified at Hornchurch as fit for travel. The conducting officer of the group was Second Lieutenant Archibald MacDonald, who had been with the Niueans throughout their army service. They were joined by 13 other sick and wounded soldiers and a nursing sister from the New Zealand hospital at Walton-on-Thames.

The ship sailed out into the Atlantic and south towards the first port of call at Dakar on the west coast of Africa. Although sea voyages were thought to be beneficial to restoring health, the Niuean men had more problems. On 23 June 1916, just before they reached Dakar, Private Peni died in the ship's hospital of pneumonia and was buried at sea that same day. A burial at sea followed a set pattern: the men gathered on one side of the ship; the captain (in this case Captain Hart) read the service and a hymn was sung; then the ship was brought to a stop and the body, wrapped in a Union Jack, was lowered over the side. The presence of Chaplain Uea on the ship meant some of the service and the hymn could be in Vagahau Niue.

There were four more burials at sea on this voyage.[2] Shortly after they left Dakar en route for Cape Town, the second death occurred – Peni's brother Sergeant Pulu, who also had acute pneumonia. The story is told on Niue that when Peni was being lowered over the ship the men were told to look away but at the last moment Pulu looked towards his brother, and his death followed soon after[3] – however it is not certain that Pulu was even on deck for the burial of his brother; he may well have been lying ill below decks, in the ship's hospital. On 27 June Private Tiueatama of Lakepa died of septic tonsillitis, and on the following day Private Vaihola of Avatele died of pneumonia and peritonitis and was buried as the ship reached the equator. Then, early in the morning on 4 July, Private Pineki of Alofi died of pneumonia and was buried at sea.

The names of the five Niueans who died at sea off the coast of Africa during the return of the Corinthic *are included on the memorial arch in Karori Servicemen's Cemetery in Wellington.* AUTHOR'S COLLECTION

The ship arrived at Cape Town, where they took on fresh supplies and fuel and notified the army authorities of the deaths that had occurred. Some men were given leave to go ashore but it is unlikely that the Niueans were among them, as the British settlers in South Africa were prepared to extend hospitality only to the Europeans on board New Zealand troopships. A New Zealand soldier who called at Durban a month later recalled how the Māori in their group were ignored at an afternoon tea party. 'We saw the Maoris were not getting anything. So we said to the ladies, "What about our friends here?" "Oh, we can't serve them." So we had to go and get the tea and cakes and take it to the Maoris. That was our first experience of South Africa.'[4]

From Cape Town the *Corinthic* set out across the Indian Ocean to Hobart, Tasmania, and here the Niueans were welcomed and entertained by the local Red Cross Society. There was special interest in the fact that so many of the men came from 'the isolated island of Niue'. Private cars and a four-horse charabanc took the visitors on a scenic tour, followed by a reception in the town hall where the men were welcomed by the governor of Tasmania, entertained and given afternoon tea:

> The Niueans sang the chorus of Tipperary with really excellent effect, the voices blending very harmoniously … The native troops, all with wattle blossom gaily decorating their hats, were then formed up outside and were marched back to the ship under a Niuean sergeant.[5]

From Hobart it was a short journey across the Tasman to Auckland, where they arrived on the evening of 6 August 1916, after seven weeks at sea. The next morning there was a reception on Queens Wharf, attended by the mayor of Auckland and civic and military officials. The most welcome sight for the Niuean men, however, would have been the gathering of Niueans resident in Auckland.

The men wrote to Captain Hart to thank him for their treatment on board *Corinthic*:

> To the captain of the ship –Our great love to you for the way you have treated us since the beginning of the voyage from England on June 17 to the end of the trip. We are very pleased for all the things that you have remembered us

The Epsom convalescent home received many of the Niueans returning from England. They had to wait here until shipping could be organised to take them home to Niue.
SIR GEORGE GREY SPECIAL COLLECTIONS, AUCKLAND LIBRARIES, NEW ZEALAND, 1-W1658 (H. WINKELMANN)

> with; we have never had to ask you for anything. You allowed us to attend the three concerts, which we all enjoyed. You arranged for deck games for us, including cricket, and which pleased us very much.
>
> We had clean white cabins and comfortable beds. We had plenty of room to walk about the deck and enjoy ourselves there. We were all very pleased with the food provided.
>
> We wish that you be blessed in every way on your various journeys. Our great love to you. To all the officers, to the doctor and to the others who toil on the ship. Our thanks to you; our love to you; our thanks for giving us plenty, for looking after us, and for your generosity at all times.[6]

After medical examinations, six men were transferred to Auckland Hospital for treatment and the remainder were divided between convalescent hospitals in Devonport and Epsom. Just as in England, homes in Auckland had been converted to serve as hospitals and convalescent homes for men returning from war. Alexander Watson offered the use of his house and grounds at Devonport:

> A more ideal spot for a convalescent home would be difficult to find. The grounds, which are about an acre in extent, are level, and laid out in lawns and gardens, while the view of the harbour, hills and city is uninterrupted. The house is an old-fashioned one, substantially built, and has wide verandahs all round it.[7]

The people of Devonport contributed to the cost of equipping the home, which could accommodate up to 24 patients. About 15 of the Niueans were sent here. The rest went to a home in Epsom: Barstow House – named after the family that had owned it, and now the property of the Auckland Hospital Board. Money for equipment was raised by the members of the Epsom nursing division of the St John Ambulance Association, and residents and schools in Epsom contributed supplies to the home. Sister Mary Worthington was matron of the home. From July to October 1916 most of the patients were Niuean. They must have made an impact on Sister Worthington – and she on them – for in the 1930s she travelled to Niue to be reacquainted with the men.[8]

Before *Corinthic* reached New Zealand, the second large group of Niueans was marched out from Hornchurch and boarded the *Arawa* for sailing on 14 July. This time the conducting officer was George Fromm who, like MacDonald, had been with the Niuean contingent since their arrival at Narrow Neck camp. He had accompanied the first group of Niueans from Egypt to France in April 1916, had been with them on the Western Front and had then accompanied them from Armentières to Etaples and Hornchurch. The instructions from the NZEF Headquarters in London to Wellington state that Fromm was sent in charge of the Niue Islanders 'for duty as interpreter'.[9] A newspaper report on his return to New Zealand said that Godley had informed Fromm that 'he would have to take them home, as he had acquired a good knowledge of the ways and habits of the Islanders'.[10]

There were no deaths on the voyage of the *Arawa* even though there were 100 men on board, including 60 Niueans. A case of measles early in the voyage was contained by isolating the patient and generally the time at sea

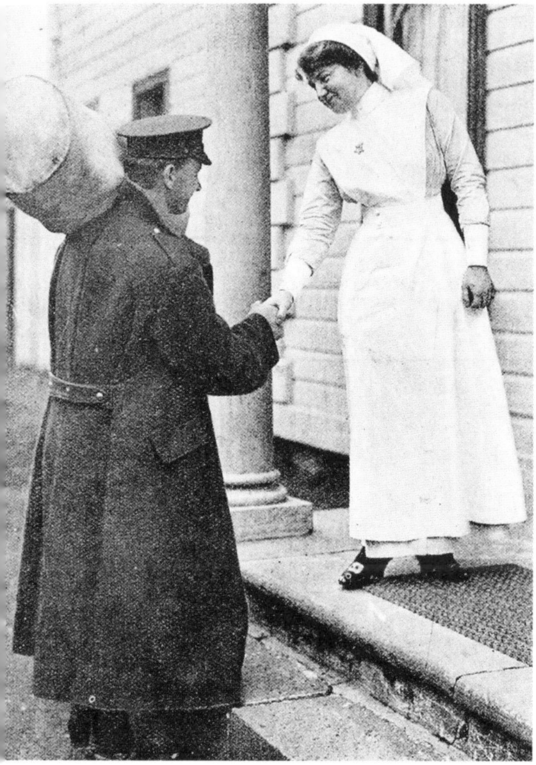

LEFT: *Sister Mary Worthington, matron in charge at the Epsom convalescent home, nursed many of the Niueans in Auckland while they waited for a ship to take them home.* SIR GEORGE GREY SPECIAL COLLECTIONS, AUCKLAND LIBRARIES, NEW ZEALAND, AWNS-19151104-48-2

RIGHT: *This group of Niueans was entertained at the Auckland Trained Nurses' Club in Epsom by Nurse Nobbs, who had worked in Rarotonga. The woman at the centre is Mrs J.H. Gunson, mayoress of Auckland, a guest at the gathering.* SIR GEORGE GREY SPECIAL COLLECTIONS, AUCKLAND LIBRARIES, NEW ZEALAND, 31_WP8025 (H.J. SCHMIDT)

was considered beneficial to the health of the servicemen. *Arawa* followed the same route as *Corinthic* to Cape Town and then to Hobart and, during the two-day stop there, the Niueans were treated to the same hospitality as the men on board *Corinthic* had been. One New Zealand soldier reportedly said of the Niueans, 'they are fine fighters but it is their lungs that won't stand the severe winter climate'.[11]

The arrival of the *Arawa* in Auckland on 3 September was the occasion for another civic reception. Five hundred people were on Queens Wharf, as was the minister of defence, Sir James Allen. The men underwent medical inspection and were then allowed to disembark – with the exception of one, Private Timoko of Hakupu, who was suffering from pulmonary tuberculosis and had to be transferred to Auckland Hospital. The others gathered for the speeches of welcome and Allen asked a Niuean soldier to interpret his comments.

Mr Allen welcomed them on behalf of the people of the Dominion, and said that he regretted that they had sustained hardships without reaching the firing-line. Their action in offering their services, he said, had won the admiration of the peoples of the British Empire.[12]

With the arrival of most of the Niueans in New Zealand, decisions had to be made about the return to their homeland. Allen was not pleased that they had been returned at all. In July 1916 he requested information about them from Godley. These two men had kept in close contact on the matter of the Niueans and until this point Godley had shown an interest in their welfare and their positioning within the New Zealand forces. His reply to Allen's letter was vague, however: 'the Niue Islanders could not stand the climate, and they practically all have drifted back either to Egypt or to NZ'.[13] The Niueans had not 'drifted' anywhere. Clear orders were given for them to be marched out from France to Hornchurch, and the only ones remaining in Egypt were the few still hospitalised. In an October letter Allen pressed Godley further:

> I can but express my extreme regret that the Niue Islanders were ever sent away from the warm climate of Egypt. It was against my grain to send them back to Niue Island before the war is over. You will remember that we distinctly requested that they should be left in Egypt because of the difficulties of climate.[14]

Godley placated the minister by agreeing that the Niueans should not have been returned home, but he said that the decision had been made by General Birdwood, who had taken the first half of the Australian and New Zealand Divisions (known as I ANZAC) to France in early April. Godley had stayed in Egypt with sections of the Australian Division still completing training (known as II ANZAC). He went to France in early June and the New Zealand Division at once transferred to his command. Thus when the decision was made to withdraw the Niueans, Birdwood was in command. Although he did not know the circumstances of the Niueans well, his decision was no doubt based on the advice he was given – especially the increasing rate of illness among the men.

Back in New Zealand the minister of defence and Defence Headquarters felt some embarrassment at having retired the Niueans from the conflict so quickly. There was discussion about what could be done with them. A suggestion to use them in Samoa, which New Zealand had occupied from the beginning of the war, was not thought useful; so the only alternative was to return them to Niue. Brigadier-General Robin explained in handwritten notes to Allen:

> I see nothing else but to return them to their homes … It would cause trouble to send them to Samoa … The Hon. M. Pomare might take them and explain the snow and ice weather … that they did well but having plenty of men used to cold winter … for sake of the island's future they are returned home.[15]

In another note he suggested that 'if they are well thanked and the unsuitability of the European climate made clear I do not consider there will be [ill] feeling'.[16]

Men from the Epsom convalescent home are served afternoon tea at the Auckland Trained Nurses' Club. ALEXANDER TURNBULL LIBRARY, WELLINGTON, NEW ZEALAND, 1/1-001567-G (H.J. SCHMIDT)

Besides the broad issue of whether the Niueans should have been returned or not there were more mundane issues to be decided, such as whether they should receive the usual three weeks' leave prior to final discharge; whether they should be issued with train passes for the leave period; and whether they should be given an issue of civilian clothing, as were other discharged soldiers. The decision was made not to issue train passes as it was thought 'not desirable that they should be allowed to travel about the Dominion; it were better that they remain in the [Epsom] Convalescent Home until they take their departure from New Zealand'.[17] They would be issued with civilian clothing, and the date of their final discharge was to be three weeks after arrival in Niue – so in fact their leave would be taken in Niue and not in New Zealand. This decision was important in determining the date up to which the men would receive pay.[18]

All that remained was to find vessels going to Niue that could transport the men home. Some were sent on the schooner *Awanui*, which was given a special dispensation to carry 10 more men than the usual limit, so long as there was a lifebelt on board for each extra person. Others travelled on the Union Steam Ship Company vessel *Talune* which did not normally call at Niue, but special arrangements were made to deliver the servicemen.[19] Most of the men arrived home in September or October 1916, approximately a year after their departure. Another group of eight men arrived in December – this included the six Niueans who had been transported from England to New Zealand on the hospital ship *Marama*. Four men were kept longer in hospitals in Egypt, France and England; they were returned to New Zealand on SS *Rotorua* in November. One of these men, Corporal Latoa of Alofi, explained how their ship took a different route: it crossed the Atlantic to Jamaica, passed through the Panama Canal, sailed north to Vancouver then south to Tahiti and Rarotonga before reaching New Zealand. Such a journey meant that these four Niueans had in fact 'been all over the World'.[20] By the time they reached Auckland in early January it was the cyclone season in the Pacific and they had to stay in Auckland until May 1917, when the first vessel travelled to Niue.

Two men were not discharged because of illness. Timoko had been taken from *Arawa* to Auckland Hospital with tuberculosis. Of the men transferred to Auckland Hospital from *Corinthic*, Private Taumataua of Lakepa was still there, also with tuberculosis. Both died in Auckland – Timoko on 21 September 1916 and Taumataua on 19 December 1916. Both were still enlisted in the New Zealand Army at the time of their death, and are buried in the servicemen's section of Waikumete Cemetery in Glen Eden, Auckland.

For the fortunate ones who survived, the return to Niue was filled with emotion. The arrival of a vessel was always an important occasion and when one arrived carrying Niuean soldiers the excitement and joy were great. There was no warning of the arrival of a vessel and when the word went out from Alofi that one was in sight and was carrying soldiers, families came from around the island to search for their men. One man later recalled: 'when [the soldiers] eventually arrived home the island greeted them to a massive feast of welcome in honour of the heroes that supported Great Britain's call for volunteers'.[21] There were stories to tell, sad news to pass on to some families, new babies to meet and, for both the families and the returning men, there was the inevitable dislocation that comes with absence to be overcome.

The Reverend Cullen, still running the LMS mission, expressed gratitude that the men had arrived back but wondered whether their behaviour would have changed: 'We are greatly pleased to get them back … I fear that those who have returned have learnt many bad ways. Since the advent of Christianity on Niue there has been no fighting. We are wondering whether hereditary instincts will be revived.'[22]

The new resident commissioner on Niue, Guy Morris, was himself a returned serviceman. In his annual report to the minister he suggested the Niueans felt an increased sense of loyalty as a result of their participation in the war:

> … even in this little island outpost the war has left its effects. There is the sadness of lonely Niuean graves in countries the names of which were hardly known hitherto to the Natives, but among the people there is also a wider knowledge of the world and of the meaning of civilization, a pride in the nation to which they belong, and an assurance that our flag is no mere empty symbol, our Empire no vain boast.[23]

For the men and their families the sentiments were more straightforward: they were simply happy to be together again.

DETAIL: *Members of the Pioneer Battalion laying a road in Messines, 1917.* ALEXANDER TURNBULL LIBRARY, WELLINGTON, NEW ZEALAND, 1/2-012772-G (H.A. SANDERS)

CHAPTER 9

Other Niueans who served with NZEF

Apart from the main body of men in the Niue contingent, from October 1915 to October 1916 there was a sprinkling of men from the island who served in other sections of the NZEF. Two left before the main body, several others saw service that partly overlapped with it, and two left the island to serve as the main body was arriving home. These men are more difficult to identify in the NZEF records, but when the resident commissioner was asked to provide names for an honours board that was being prepared in New Zealand in the 1920s, seven extra names and their service numbers were forwarded to Wellington.[1]

Five of these were Niueans who were living and working in New Zealand when war began in 1914, or were working on ships that serviced the Pacific Islands out of the port of Auckland. Hono Paufai was working for a hairdresser in Queen Street, Auckland,[2] Mick Haller was a cook in an Auckland hotel and Jack Harrys worked in a flaxmill on the Coromandel Peninsula. Make Allan was a crew member on the sailing vessel *Ysabel* that sailed regularly between Auckland and Niue, and William Alfred was cook on the Union Steam Ship Company vessel SS *Kauri*. They would all have been at least reasonably proficient in English.

Niueans on the island generally went by a single name. Those who had moved to work in New Zealand found this was a difficulty and they added a second name, perhaps that of their father or another close family relative, or they took a Pālagi surname or a whole new name. Like Puleua, who changed his name to Purie Davi Harry (see chapter 4), Neki enlisted as Make Allan and Patali as Mick Haller.[3]

The first Niueans to enlist were William Alfred in December 1914 and Hono Paufai in January 1915; both were placed in the Auckland Infantry Battalion. Private Alfred sailed with the 3rd Reinforcements in February 1915 and Private Paufai followed in May as part of the 5th Reinforcements; both were destined for Egypt, then on to Gallipoli. Alfred disembarked at Suez in late March 1915 and was on the Gallipoli peninsula early in the conflict there. During action in late May he received light shrapnel wounds to the head; he was treated by the Field Ambulance staff and returned to duty in June.

Paufai arrived in Egypt at the end of May. After training for two months, the 5th Reinforcements were sent on to support the Auckland Infantry Battalion on the slopes of Gallipoli in August 1915.

Both Paufai and Alfred were involved in the second major offensive at Gallipoli, known as Sari Bair, which began on 6 August 1915. The Auckland Battalion attacked Chunuk Bair, where they were met with intense Ottoman machine-gun and rifle fire and suffered 300 casualties. Alfred received gunshot wounds to his arm and wrist. The 5th Reinforcements arrived on the peninsula during the attack; they were rowed ashore and went straight into battle. 'Theirs was a most unenviable situation. Some lasted no time at all. Others were wounded making their way up Rhododendron Spur … their Gallipoli service was reckoned in hours, not days.'[4] Paufai reached the heights of Hill 971 on the Sari Bair range before he received gunshot wounds to his chest.

It needed six men to get a stretcher down from the high slopes and then there was a long, difficult carry for two or four men, often under sniper fire, to the casualty clearing station near the beach. Those soldiers who survived the evacuation were transported out to hospital ships and transferred to the British hospital at Malta or hospitals in Egypt, depending on their condition.

Alfred was taken down the slopes and out to the hospital ship *Delta* for transport to Egypt. His injury was not life-threatening but needed treatment and he was admitted to the Australian General Hospital at Heliopolis on the outskirts of Cairo. He spent six weeks there before he was sent back to New Zealand. It would be another six months before he was declared no longer fit for war service and was discharged from the NZEF.[5]

Wounded soldiers at a casualty clearing station on the Gallipoli peninsula wait for evacuation. Hono Paufai and William Alfred were brought down the slopes by stretcher in August 1915 and were transferred to hospital ships in the bay beyond.
ALEXANDER TURNBULL LIBRARY, WELLINGTON, NEW ZEALAND, PA1-O-863-03-5

Paufai was taken to the British hospital in Malta where he was classed as 'seriously ill with gunshot wound to chest' and shipped on to England. He entered the King George Hospital in London in late August. The King George – formerly HM Stationery Office near Waterloo Station – was reportedly the largest hospital in the UK. Commandeered for use as a Red Cross military hospital, the relatively new building was rapidly converted and opened in time to cope with the thousands being evacuated from the Dardanelles. The wounded were brought by boat-train from the south coast to Waterloo Station and then taken through tunnels that had been built to enable stationery supplies to be easily moved. This meant Londoners were spared the sight of badly wounded servicemen arriving in large numbers.

Sybil Lee, in her capacity as 'official Maori visitor' for the NZWCA, was directed to this hospital to visit 'the one or two Maoris' who had been invalided from Gallipoli and here she made a surprising discovery:

> Last year [1915], in one of the largest of the London Military Hospitals, three boys fought a desperate battle for life, from August to well into December. One, shot through his only sound lung, went to the very door of death time and again: doctors and nurses saw no hope for him; there were times he couldn't speak, but he always managed a smile, and only needed to hear how sisters and nurses spoke of him to see the high opinion they had formed – and it was a source of great joy to all connected with that ward, that he was able, though a shadow of his former self, to enter into the Christmas festivities. By the way, he is a Niue Islander.[6]

The man was Hono Paufai. After six long months he was considered fit to be invalided back to New Zealand. He sailed for Suez from southern England on 15 March 1916, the day the main body of Niue men disembarked at Suez. By the time the ship reached Suez, he had contracted pleurisy and was admitted to the New Zealand General Hospital at Pont de Koubbeh – the very hospital where increasing numbers of Niueans from the main body were being sent as they succumbed to pneumonia or dysentery.

In mid-April Paufai was invalided back to Auckland and admitted to Auckland Hospital. For the next two and a half years he was in and out of hospital, and he died at the hospital annex in November 1918, five days before the war ended. Paufai was buried in the servicemen's section of Waikumete Cemetery.[7]

It is possible that William Alfred returned to his father, Pilitasi, in Tuapa for at least a time. Reverend Cullen was referring to Alfred when he wrote in 1916:

> We are extremely proud of one man, who was among the Anzacs in the landing on April 25th, who was twice wounded at Gallipoli, and is now retired on pension and with a crippled arm. Even little Niue has her share in the glory of that gallant though unavailing enterprise.[8]

Alfred continued to work as a seaman in spite of his injury and lived to the age of 85. He is buried in Waikumete and his name appears on the Tuapa war memorial as Viliamu Afele, a transliteration of the English name.

While Alfred was recovering in Auckland and Paufai was lying seriously ill in London, another Niuean enlisted in Auckland. Make Allan of Tamakautoga worked on the sailing vessel *Ysabel*, which did regular freight runs between

Private Hono Paufai was seriously wounded at Gallipoli. He spent six months in hospital in England before being invalided back to New Zealand. He died in Auckland five days before the war ended. SIR GEORGE GREY SPECIAL COLLECTIONS, AUCKLAND LIBRARIES, NEW ZEALAND, *AUCKLAND STAR* 30 SEPTEMBER 1915

Auckland and Niue. When the *Ysabel* arrived in Auckland in November 1915, he left the vessel and enlisted in the NZEF. He was 22 years old.

At the time of his enlistment, the 150 men comprising the Niue contingent had recently entered Narrow Neck camp in Auckland for training. It might have been expected that Private Allan would be sent to join them but instead he was attached to the New Zealand Medical Corps and, four days after his medical clearance was obtained and without any training in New Zealand, he was en route for the Middle East – to a war service that was unlike anything experienced by any other Niuean.

The reason for this seems to be his experience as a crewman on the *Ysabel* and possibly on other vessels. Earlier in 1915 a passenger vessel had been converted to a hospital ship, NZHS *Maheno*, and sent to the Mediterranean to

Private Make Allan enlisted in Auckland in November 1915; he was placed in the New Zealand Medical Corps and served as a crew member on the new hospital ship Marama.*He then served as a stretcher bearer in Egypt and on the Western Front for nearly two years. At the Battle of Passchendaele in October 1917, Make Allan received gunshot wounds and had to be evacuated. He received hospital treatment in France, England and back in Auckland, but died in June 1918.* COURTESY OF MRS JANE IKIHEGA AND FAMILY, NEW ZEALAND help evacuate men from Gallipoli. Now another hospital ship was needed, and a second speedy conversion was undertaken to prepare NZHS *Marama* for service. When Allan enlisted and was identified as someone with experience as a seaman, he was immediately taken on as a crew member on the *Marama*. The ship sailed from New Zealand on 5 December 1915 with him on board.

When the *Marama* reached Suez on 11 January 1916, Allan was sent to the New Zealand General Hospital at Koubbeh. The Medical Corps needed staff as stretcher bearers for the Field Ambulance units. Allan served in No. 3 Field Ambulance for 18 months, first in Egypt, and then he went with the main movement of New Zealand troops from Egypt to France in April 1916. Many others from the Niue contingent were involved in this move, too, but there is no record of whether Allan met any of his fellow Niueans.

In the north of France the three NZ Field Ambulance units were each attached to an infantry brigade. With around 300 men, the field ambulance provided stretcher bearers to carry the badly wounded between the first-aid posts and the dressing stations. During major actions they also went out into the battlefield to find the wounded and bring them in. The work was physically and emotionally draining, and dangerous. In the north of France many stretcher bearers were killed or wounded or gassed. The men they collected had hideous injuries and often died in their care. They had to make choices as to who they lifted out; the worst cases they left to their fate. The countryside in the north of France became a moonscape of shell holes filled with water and mud, and lifting and carrying in these conditions was physically exhausting.

Make Allan worked with the field ambulance service in France through until October 1917, with a few weeks' leave in England in July 1917. In October 1917 he was part of the No. 3 Field Ambulance attached to the NZ Rifle Brigade that was involved in the third Battle of Ypres, known as Passchendaele. The attack took place on 12 October and became New Zealand's most disastrous day of World War I; the New Zealanders suffered 3700 casualties, including 800 dead, without taking a single objective.

Among those casualties was Make Allan. He received gunshot wounds to his right leg, causing a compound fracture and considerable blood loss, and he

An advanced dressing station on the Western Front. As a stretcher bearer Allan was part of a team who went out into the battlefield to carry the wounded back to aid posts and dressing stations. It was difficult work, both physically and emotionally.
ALEXANDER TURNBULL LIBRARY, WELLINGTON, NEW ZEALAND, 1/2-012928-G

was now dependent on the people he had served with. Evacuated by stretcher to a casualty clearing station, he was assessed as needing surgery and sent on to the 5th British General Hospital in Rouen. He was operated on and received several blood transfusions and, after 10 days there, was transferred by ambulance train and then by HS *Panama* across the Channel and into the Royal Victoria Hospital at Netley. In February 1918 he was transferred to the nearby No. 1 New Zealand General Hospital at Brockenhurst and was soon placed on the seriously ill list. As well as being an important surgical hospital, Brockenhurst had become the New Zealand specialist shell shock treatment centre in England, and it is possible that by this time Allan was suffering the effects of what he had witnessed on the Western Front.

On 6 April 1918 he was embarked on the NZHS *Marama* for the return to New Zealand and on arrival in Auckland was admitted to Avondale Mental

Jack Harrys from Lakepa was at first enlisted into the Auckland Mounted Rifles and appeared in this group photo taken in Egypt soon after arrival. Harrys is on the left in the first row of men standing – the only Polynesian face in the group. By the time this photo appeared in print in New Zealand he had been transferred to the Maori Contingent, which was being reorganised as the Pioneer Battalion. SIR GEORGE GREY SPECIAL COLLECTIONS, AUCKLAND LIBRARIES, NEW ZEALAND, AWNS-19160203-45-1

Hospital. The medical board noted that, in addition to his leg injuries, he was suffering from tuberculosis and also 'mental derangement': the medical report stated that his disability was 'clearly attributable to service during the present war'. Make Allan died on 25 June 1918 and was buried in the servicemen's section at Waikumete Cemetery.[9]

Two other Niueans who were working in New Zealand when war began both served with the Pioneer Battalion on the Western Front, but not at the same time. Jack Harrys, from the village of Lakepa, was working on the Coromandel Peninsula southeast of Auckland. He was part of a group that was sent to Wellington in June 1915 and enlisted at Trentham Camp. He was assigned to the Auckland Mounted Rifles and was therefore given the rank of trooper rather than private. He sailed for Egypt in August 1915 and, later in the year, was transferred to the Maori Contingent, which was being reorganised after the withdrawal from Gallipoli. When the main body of the NZEF left Port Said for Marseilles on 7 April 1916, Harrys was part of the 976-strong Pioneer Battalion that also included 60 members of the Niuean contingent. Like so many of the Niueans, Harrys found climatic conditions in the north of France very difficult and he spent most of May in hospital with pleurisy. However he recovered and, just after the main body of Niueans was marched out for England, he was returned to his battalion.

The Pioneers now became part of the Somme offensive. They moved onto the Somme battlefield to prepare vital communication trenches:

> The Pioneers found themselves billeted among the South African and German dead in Delville Wood. The ground was a muddy horror with the woods marked by the bared stumps of splintered trees. Shelling went on day and night, gas shells being mixed with the shrapnel and high explosives … The platoons worked in relays under gas and shell fire that produced a steady trickle of casualties.[10]

One of those casualties was Jack Harrys on 29 September. He was evacuated to the No. 1 Canadian General Hospital in Rouen with gunshot wounds to the back and head and was then transported by ambulance train and hospital ship and arrived in the 2nd London General Hospital in Chelsea. Three months later he was sent to convalesce at Hornchurch but then, in March 1917, he was

Mick Haller, Patali, of Alofi North. Haller was sent with the 13th Maori Reinforcements in early 1917. He joined the Pioneers in Western France and served with them until the end of the war. He returned to Niue after the war and became a village councillor.
AUTHOR'S COLLECTION

Members of the Pioneer Battalion laying a road in Messines, 1917. It was a slow and laborious task, but men and equipment had to be moved towards the front. ALEXANDER TURNBULL LIBRARY, WELLINGTON, NEW ZEALAND, 1/2-012772-G (H.A. SANDERS)

admitted to the No. 3 New Zealand General Hospital at Codford with pneumonia. He remained for weeks on the seriously ill list and it was not until July 1917 that he was well enough to be embarked for New Zealand on the hospital ship *Marama* and then admitted to the sanatorium in Rotorua for in-patient treatment for tuberculosis. In late October 1917 he was discharged from the New Zealand Forces as unfit for duty.[11] It is unknown whether he returned to Niue at all, but he appears to have finally settled in the Wellington area.

Mick Haller enlisted in June 1916. He trained at Narrow Neck and was part of the 13th Maori Reinforcements who departed for England in January 1917. On arrival, Private Haller was assigned to Sling Camp on the Salisbury Plains. In this large training camp for New Zealand soldiers, his experience as a cook was needed and he worked there for the next six months before being transferred to France and joining the Pioneer Battalion in the field. The Pioneers had just become a full Māori unit and given the title New Zealand Maori

(Pioneer) Battalion. They were heavily involved at Passchendaele, trying to keep the roads open by laying planks to give the guns traction, 'but this, like Passchendaele itself, was a lost cause'.[12] As Mick Haller worked to move men and equipment forward, Make Allan was working to take the wounded back behind the lines to the dressing stations.

Christmas 1917 was spent in the mud of France, and during the advance of 1918 the Pioneers kept roads open, repaired bridges and filled bomb craters. Armistice came on 11 November 1918 but there was still work to do, and Haller was among the Pioneers as they trekked towards the German border. There they were halted and an earlier order to proceed to Cologne was cancelled by the British authorities, who 'deemed it inappropriate to have a European country occupied by indigenous soldiers'.[13] This meant the Maori Pioneers were now repatriated via Dunkirk and England. Haller returned to New Zealand with the main body of the Maori (Pioneer) Battalion and witnessed the huge welcome given at Auckland when the troopship *Westmoreland* arrived. He was one of only a small number of Niuean men who came through their ordeal without illness or injury.[14]

Two Pālagi, Ernest Cunningham and Alfred Godsmark, who had moved to Niue to work and had married Niuean women, also served in the NZEF and were included in the resident commissioner's list for the Niue Island Roll of Honour board. Cunningham was born in Auckland in 1873. He went to Niue in 1891, initially to work for the trader Edwin Nicholas in his store at Utuko and later for Robert Head in Mutalau. He was given the Niuean name of Misi Ene. He married Fafili in 1910 and was present to farewell her two brothers, Pimeleko and Talauta, when they left with the contingent in October 1915.

Alfred Godsmark, who had immigrated from Lincolnshire to New Zealand, arrived on Niue in about 1908; he, too, worked for Head in a trading store – this one in Avatele – and married Ahome from that village.

OVER PAGE: *Men from the Pioneer Battalion making a road between war-damaged buildings in France, 1918.*
ALEXANDER TURNBULL LIBRARY, WELLINGTON, NEW ZEALAND, 1/2-013793-G (H.A. SANDERS)

H1246

Cunningham and Godsmark sailed together from Niue in October 1916 as the main body of Niueans were being welcomed home. They enlisted in Auckland: Private Godsmark went into the Auckland Infantry Battalion, and Private Cunningham was sent to Trentham and attached to the Wellington Regiment. Cunningham applied for reimbursement of travelling expenses, £6 10s, incurred in coming to camp from Niue. The army paymaster was reluctant to meet these costs, given that Cunningham had come to New Zealand on his own initiative, but when Dr Pomare, minister for the Cook and other Islands, was asked to comment, he said, 'when at Niue I appealed not only to the Natives but also to the few eligible Europeans to go to NZ if possible and enlist'. Cunningham got his refund.[15]

Both men left New Zealand in early 1917 and when they arrived in England they were marched into Sling Camp for further training. They were both moved to active service in France in June 1917, but from that point their experiences diverged. Godsmark was the victim of a gas attack in September 1917 and was carried to a casualty clearing station by the 3rd Field Ambulance, in which Make Allan was still serving. He was sent by hospital ship to England and it was eight months before he was discharged back to New Zealand. Cunningham was soon withdrawn behind the lines to work in the Employment Company; he was 44, and the medical board found him 'too aged' for active service. Both men were returned to New Zealand in early 1918 and to Niue later that year.[16]

The well-known trader on Niue, Robert Henry Head, also had one son who served in the NZEF. Head had been shipwrecked on Niue in 1867 and had married a local woman, Pelenise of Alofi. Their youngest son Charles had been living in New Zealand for 20 years when he enlisted in 1917 and was placed in the Otago Regiment. He saw service in England and France before returning to New Zealand in early 1919. Given the prominence of his father on Niue it is perhaps surprising that the name of Charles Head was not added to the resident commissioner's list in 1926 for inclusion on the honours board – even though he had lived away from the island for many years.[17]

By the time the Armistice was signed in northern France on 11 November 1918, the only Niuean still serving with the NZEF was Mick Haller who was with the Maori (Pioneer) Battalion at Le Quesnoy in the northeast of France. Of the 160 Niuean men who had served, 24 of them – 15 per cent – were dead. Their journey to war was marked by headstones and marble tablets in New Zealand, Egypt, France, England and Niue. A few of the survivors were in New Zealand but the majority were back on Nukutūtaha, the island that stands alone.

In February 1920 a New Zealand parliamentary delegation led by the minister of defence, Sir James Allen, arrived to officially thank the people of Niue for their contribution to the war effort. Allen unveiled a memorial and presented a captured German field gun. ARCHIVES NEW ZEALAND, THE DEPARTMENT OF INTERNAL AFFAIRS TE TARI TAIWHENUA, IT1 ITT 122/3

CHAPTER 10

The aftermath of war

As the Armistice was being signed, a new terror struck – the influenza pandemic. Starting in early 1918 it spread around the world to become one of the deadliest natural disasters ever.

The Pacific region was not spared: four days before the ceasefire agreement was signed on 11 November the *Talune* arrived in New Zealand-administered Samoa from Auckland. Despite evidence of influenza among the passengers and crew, all were permitted to disembark, and by the time the bonfires were lit along the waterfront in Apia to celebrate the ending of war in Europe, the first victims of the influenza pandemic were dying.

Everywhere there was illness and death.[1] The disease devastated Samoa: 22 per cent of the population died.[2] The vessel had already called in at Fiji, and it went on from Samoa to Tonga, Nauru and back to Fiji. All these islands were badly affected. In New Zealand the death toll in late 1918 was 8600; those who were still in military camps were especially vulnerable. In Tahiti 13 per cent of the population died. An outbreak in Rarotonga in September 1918 resulted in 45 deaths, but fast quarantine restrictions meant the outer Cook Islands were spared. Niue was also spared; for once the irregularity of shipping was a blessing.

It is not clear when exactly the news reached Niue that Europe was at peace, although it was probably around Christmas when the schooner *Awanui* arrived from Auckland. There was much celebrating and the resident commissioner reported: 'steps are being taken to celebrate Peace Day in a fitting manner. Besides speeches and festivities in the various villages, every person on the island will plant a coconut and these trees will serve as a constant reminder of the war and its significance.'[3] Some villages set aside a piece of land in their village as a 'Peace Plantation',[4] and others planted trees along the roadside or in the usual plantation; in all, over 15,000 coconuts were planted. The resident commissioner suggested the tree-planting be repeated in future years to mark the anniversary. He also noted that the returned soldiers played a big part in the festivities held in the villages.

The end of the war meant that efforts to train a second contingent on Niue could be concluded without any men being sent away.[5] The plan had been to train this group for Palestine, where the Rarotongan Company had been serving since late 1916.[6] Although there may have been a desire on Niue to contribute further it is unlikely that this offer would have been accepted, even if the war had continued. When the main body of Niueans was brought back from England and returned to Niue, the minister of defence was asked to 'make a statement regarding the future policy of the [Defence] Department in connection with the Niue Islanders, seeing that those already trained have had such a trying time at the front':

> The Hon. Mr Allen (Minister of Defence) replied that he did not think it would be wise in the future to accept any more men from Niue Island for active service abroad, the reason being that they might have to go to a climate that was not at all suitable to them. Although he thought it was right to have made the experiment, he did not think it would be carried any further.[7]

The widespread illness among the Niueans was a concern, and there was the issue of transporting the men to New Zealand for training and returning them to Niue after service – which entailed chartering or diverting a vessel to call at the island, at great cost to the government.

A principle of equality of pay for all members of the NZEF was enforced from the outset of the war. It was reinforced in 1918 when New Zealand accepted, at the request of the British government, a group of 25 men of the Gilbert Native Police from the British colony of the Gilbert and Ellice Islands. When it was discovered that their pay was considerably less than their European comrades, the New Zealand government decided to increase their pay and meet the costs. Allen pointed out at the time that within the NZEF there were Europeans, Māori, Niueans and Cook Islanders all drawing the same standard rates of pay, and other Pacific Islanders should be treated equally.[8] Likewise, it was policy that men should be returned home at the end of their service, and while this was an expensive undertaking in the case of the Niue men and of the Gilbert Islanders, it was considered a necessary expense.

On Niue, finalising the pay, separation allowances and war gratuities proved to be a lengthy and involved process, not because the principle was questioned but because of the practical difficulties of communication with the island, problems with Niuean names, ignorance of Pacific geography and the absence of a banking service on Niue. The fact that there were no formal birth and marriage certificates meant applications for separation allowances had to be coordinated by the office of the resident commissioner; his signature on each sheet of applications was taken as legal proof.[9] Henry Cornwall signed and sent the applications at the start of 1917 and, in June 1917, he wrote again to say that 'the people are growing restless and impatient at the long delay which has taken place'.[10] Arrangements were eventually made for the money to be paid into the Niue Island Administration account and it was then paid out by the resident commissioner's office. Some correspondence went to the Cook Islands and had to be returned to Wellington, and the war had in fact concluded before pay and separation allowances were finally settled.

Similarly, the payment of war gratuities to the Niue men was a slow process. This was a payment made to individual servicemen and women or their dependents after the war and was calculated according to their length of service both at home and abroad, based on a rate of one shilling and sixpence per day, in recognition of the service they had given to the country. Some gratuity payments for Niueans were still being finalised after the War Expenses Department had closed but this was mainly because the men concerned had moved off the island and were difficult to trace. Private Tafana, for example, had moved to American Samoa and it was not until mid-1927 that his gratuity of £41 2s 0d was forwarded to him.[11]

The payment of such gratuities was in sharp contrast to the policy in the British crown colony of Fiji. Here the Fiji Native Labour Corps, who had served for over a year on the docks in Calais and Marseilles, were declared

The marble tablet mounted on the war memorial on the Alofi green was made in New Zealand in 1919. It displays the names of the men from Niue who died while enlisted in the NZEF, but Private Vilipati, who died at Narrow Neck during training in late 1915, is not included. Make Allan is included under the name his family knew him as: Neki (spelt Neke on the tablet). The concrete war memorial has been replaced twice but each time the original marble tablet has been reused. AUTHOR'S COLLECTION

ineligible for a war gratuity, although a gratuity was paid to the Third Fiji Contingent – European servicemen who went only as far as England before the war ended.[12]

Some families on Niue had to come to terms with the fact that their men were not coming home and that they now lay in a foreign country. A journalist in New Zealand imagined what this might be like:

> Vasau and Taleva came from the farthest corner of the Pacific to fight for the King of England. [They] came from Niue … In Niue there are gravestones all along the roadside, for every Savage Islander is buried on his own land. But Vasau and Taleva will not be buried on their own land. Instead they are sleeping peacefully at the far end of the earth.[13]

More recently, Niuean Talava Tuhipa-Turner imagined the anguish her family must have felt:

> Two of my mother's great-uncles, Pulu and Pene, were lost during the journey from England back to Niue, causing their mother to change her name from Fukesifa to Lisiua ('throw two') in remembrance of her beloved sons who were laid to rest at sea … The effects of war are never limited to the soldiers who fight in battles. We must also remember the strong women and children left behind to provide [for] and maintain the family and the grief they encountered, like Fukesifa/Lisiua, when told their sons, partners or fathers would never return.[14]

By 1919 thoughts turned to the construction of a memorial to honour those who had not returned from the conflict. A marble tablet bearing the names of those who died during service was prepared in New Zealand and a memorial was constructed on the Alofi green. In February 1920 a parliamentary delegation arrived from New Zealand to thank the Niueans officially for their efforts. The delegation was headed by Minister of Defence Sir James Allen, and included members of both houses of the New Zealand parliament. They 'landed at Niue in the ship's boats after a precarious passage through a narrow breach in a dangerous reef, the waves breaking heavily';[15] several of them were traumatised by this, judging from their subsequent accounts.

The arrival of the group was a complete surprise as no ship had visited for three months. Messengers were quickly dispatched to all the villages asking returned soldiers to come to Alofi the next day. All mustered on the green, where Allen addressed them and presented them with £1000 from the New Zealand Red Cross in gratitude for donations received from the island for the war funds: the money was to go towards building the first hospital in Alofi. Allen also presented the Islanders with a captured German field gun, which was to be mounted on a concrete platform alongside the monument that had already been built. The list of names on the memorial, while it included Hono Paufai and Make Allan who had both served in other parts of the NZEF, did not include Vilipate, the first man in the Niuean contingent to have died while enlisted in the NZEF.

All men who served in the 1914–18 war received a scroll detailing their service: the years, theatres of war where they served and medals awarded. Many scrolls issued to Niuean men have not survived the harsh climate on Niue, but this one for 16/1069 Private Lui of Alofi was displayed at the centennial commemorations on the island in 2015.
AUTHOR'S COLLECTION

The families of men who died during the Great War received a commemorative plaque, commonly called a 'dead man's penny'. These were issued throughout the United Kingdom and empire. This one for 16/1098 Muimatagi of Mutalau, who died in 1919 following his return to Niue, is evidence that his death was recognised as being directly due to war service. It has been mounted by Muimatagi's family and was displayed at the centennial commemorations on Niue in 2015.
AUTHOR'S COLLECTION

The Niue men were recognised with war medals, too – another lengthy process, as most medals were addressed to 'Niue, Cook Islands' and were therefore sent to the resident commissioner in Rarotonga, who redirected them to Wellington for forwarding to Niue; this took several months. The men of the Niue contingent received the British War Medal and the Victory Medal. William Alfred, Hono Paufai, Make Allan and Jack Harrys also received the 1914–15 Star. All the men received a scroll detailing their service, and for the families of the men who had died in service there was a memorial plaque or medallion, commonly referred to as 'a dead man's penny'.

A Roll of Honour that listed the names of all men who had served from Niue was prepared in New Zealand: it took the form of two wooden panels with the names written in gold leaf, enclosed in a wooden frame. In May 1926 the governor-general, Sir Charles Fergusson, came ashore at Alofi from HMS *Diomede* to unveil the honours board, which had been hung in the church in Alofi. All returned servicemen assembled at the wharf wearing their white Sunday suits and proudly bearing their war medals. During the reception at the schoolhouse at Tufukia the governor-general delivered a message from King George V, and he quoted the message from the Niueans to the King at the outbreak of war: 'I am the island of Niue, a small child that stands up to help.' The newly completed hospital was inspected, a memorial service was held in the church at Alofi and 'a huge tablet containing the names of Niueans who went to war was unveiled'.[16] The only disappointment was for those men who had been returned to Niue directly from Narrow Neck: their service was not recognised on the Roll of Honour.

For the men and their families the process of settling back into civilian life must have been difficult. Within five years of their return to the island another 10 servicemen had died from pneumonia or tuberculosis – or both.[17] Most had been hospitalised while serving overseas, and all had been medically assessed in Auckland on their return as having an ongoing chest debility caused by war service. Although this was frequently dismissed as the result of 'lack of stamina', the medical board usually agreed that the man should be 'considered' for a war pension.[18] When the infamous German raider Count

In 1926 Governor-General Sir Charles Fergusson visited Niue to unveil the new honours board hung in the Alofi church. Here he bends down to receive a gift from a small girl. To the left of the photo is a man in full army uniform, probably Sergeant Major Uea.
COURTESY OF HAMILTON FAMILY, NEW ZEALAND

Felix von Luckner made a brief call at Niue in August 1917 he noted that there were men on the wharf who had been in the trenches of northern France and that the Niueans told him, 'our men come back sick with cough. Cough never goes away.'[19] These were all young men and it is very likely their premature deaths were the result of their war service.

Two men resumed work on ships that took them to New Zealand, where they were caught in the flu pandemic of 1918. Private Makafitu of Mutalau was in Auckland when he became ill, and although he is buried at Waikumete Cemetery, he is not in the servicemen's section. Private Kulupa of Hikutavake was on a vessel that docked at Lyttelton in the South Island in November 1918, and was admitted to the casualty ward of the local hospital after 'succumbing to influenza'. He died just after the Armistice and a funeral was held for him at the Church of England in Lyttelton on 16 November. In recognition of the fact that this man, a Niue Islander, was the first returned soldier to be buried in the church cemetery, there was a special service attended by a party of returned soldiers, a firing party and representatives from the Marine Department, the Union Steam Ship Company and Military Headquarters staff: a salute was fired and the Last Post sounded.[20]

A leading figure in the Niue Contingent, Sergeant Major Uea continued to be an influential figure on the island until his death in 1947. In 2015 his family erected a new headstone at his burial site in Alofi North. AUTHOR'S COLLECTION

Some returned servicemen on Niue became LMS pastors, and at least two served in other parts of the Pacific. Private Poimatagi of Hakupu, himself the son of a pastor, entered the LMS training college at Vailahi in Alofi a few years after returning from war service. He completed four years of study before leaving with his wife in 1927 to serve at the mission in New Guinea but never returned for, like many other Niueans and Cook Islanders who served at this mission, he died of malaria. Private Taveli of Avatele became pastor for the Niuean community resident in Apia. He served at Aai o Niue village in Apia, Western Samoa, from 1940 to 1952.

Servicemen often became village leaders and were representatives on the Island Council. Sergeant Major Uea, the army chaplain, was island councillor for Alofi North from 1918 to 1922. He was an acknowledged leader on the island and was often quoted when groups visited from New Zealand. At least nine former servicemen served as island councillors; Private Tionetini of Tamakautoga served five terms.[21] Private Tohovaka of Makefu became a police sergeant on Niue and featured in Anzac Day services once they were established. He received the British Empire Medal for his services, and he was chosen, along with Malama Head, to represent the island at a reception in New Zealand for the new queen Elizabeth II in late 1953.

Private Fohetaha visited New Zealand in 1920 and was a passenger back to Niue in August of that year on the trading steamer *Jubilee*; the ship disappeared without trace somewhere en route. Private Latoa of Hakupu became a well-known boxer on Niue and later moved to Samoa and then to Tonga, where he continued with competitive boxing. Lance Corporal Tagimau and Private Lui, both of Alofi, moved to Samoa to work; both are buried in the Magiagi cemetery in Apia.[22] Several men moved in later life to Auckland and now lie in cemeteries such as Waikumete, Onehunga and Mangere.

Corporal Tefatumoana of Liku appears not to have been Niuean in the first place. He was born in Tahiti in 1893 of Tahitian parents, and learnt French at school; a relative brought him to Niue when he was about 13 years old. When he enlisted on Niue he answered 'yes' to the question, 'Are you a British subject?'. After the war he settled in New Zealand, used various names, was described as a Tahitian labourer, registered as an alien during World War II and finally, in the 1940s, applied successfully for naturalisation as a British subject. He married into a Māori family and lived happily in the Thames area.[23] He did serve in the Niuean contingent, however, and is remembered on the Liku village memorial and the national memorial.

Ernest Cunningham and Alfred Godsmark had both returned to the island in late 1918 to their family and village life, and resumed their work as traders. In Avatele Godsmark built a large Pālagi house and filled it with imported furniture for his growing family. But ongoing health problems related to his having been gassed in France forced him to move back to Auckland in late 1929 for medical treatment; he died there in May 1930 and was buried in the servicemen's section of Waikumete Cemetery. The Godsmark family moved back and forth between Niue and Auckland as various children went to school at Queen Victoria School for Maori Girls and St Stephen's College for Maori

In 1935 Sister Mary Worthington, who had cared for many of the men at the Epsom convalescent home, arrived to renew her friendships. She was photographed in Alofi with the men who had assembled on the village green to greet her. The man standing directly behind Sister Worthington is Captain William Moody Bell, resident commissioner at the time.
HUANAKI CULTURAL CENTRE AND MUSEUM, NIUE (ORIGINALS DESTROYED IN CYCLONE HETA 2004. THIS COPY FROM THE AUTHOR'S COLLECTION)

Boys. Godsmark's wife Ahome may finally have settled in Auckland, too, and from there she was eligible to apply for a war widow's pension.[24] Cunningham remained in Mutalau; when he died in 1943 he had been resident on Niue for 52 years. He is buried near the village monument in Mutalau and his name appears on that memorial as C. Ene (Cunningham Ernest).

For a long time, members of the Niue contingent who remained on Niue were often seen as a group. In 1935 Sister Worthington from the Epsom convalescent home visited Niue to renew her acquaintance with the men she had cared for in Auckland. The men assembled to greet her. They had dressed well for the occasion in their church suits and one man wore full

Visit by the governor-general, Sir Arthur Porritt, in September 1969. Alongside the second war memorial on Alofi green, he chats to returned servicemen who are proudly wearing their medals. Waiting in front of the memorial are the resident commissioner Selwyn Wilson, his wife Cecily and members of the viceregal party. A New Zealand frigate lies offshore.
AUTHOR'S COLLECTION, COURTESY OF THE LATE SELWYN WILSON, WAIKANAE

uniform and sun helmet – although he had dispensed with the boots that had been the object of so much hardship. By the 1960s their numbers were declining, but 28 of the returned servicemen gathered on the Alofi green to welcome Governor-General Sir Bernard Fergusson and his family in 1964. He had arrived to unveil a new war memorial on the island – the original one on the green had deteriorated in the harsh island climate, and a new concrete plinth had been constructed for the marble tablet. The 1959 cyclone had destroyed the church in Alofi where the original honours board had hung. In the aftermath of the cyclone Robert Rex had looked through the church wreckage and rescued some sections of the board;[25] these were stored in the Fale Fono and were put on display again in the Huanaki Cultural Centre in the late 1990s. In 2004 cyclone Heta destroyed Huanaki but two small pieces

The local newspaper on Niue, Tohi Tala Niue, *recorded in 1980 that the Anzac service that year 'had a sad and memorable beginning' with a dawn service. 'Only four veterans were able to participate', but there were also many family members representing those who had passed away. The veterans are, from left, Liuvaie, Tagamaka, Misikoni and Tio Tagevili.*
ALEXANDER TURNBULL LIBRARY, WELLINGTON, NEW ZEALAND, *TOHI TALA NIUE*, 2 MAY 1980

of the board were once again rescued and are now in Tāoga Niue, the Niue museum and cultural centre.

Although there was no Niuean contingent sent to the Second World War, individual Niueans had enlisted in New Zealand and, soon after that war ended, an Anzac Day service was begun on Niue. Expatriate New Zealander Percy Walsh, who had come to the island to work in the Public Works Department, was instrumental in starting a Dawn Parade on 25 April 1947, the year the first village memorial was built in Mutalau. The Island Council designated

Anzac Day a public holiday in 1949, and established a format for commemoration with activities centred on the returned servicemen and their families.

At first the resident commissioner, Hector Larsen, provided a government truck to go round the island and collect the returned servicemen. Later in the 1950s, Arumaki Strickland made his bus available. The men were brought to Alofi and spent the eve of Anzac Day in the administration shed on the wharf or in Araura Hall in Alofi North, where Strickland ran a cinema. They practised marching under the watchful eye of Sergeant Tohovaka, told stories, sang songs and kept memories alive. During the night families prepared wreaths to lay on the memorial the next morning, and children and grandchildren listened as the stories of the Niue contingent were passed on to the following generations. Private Taveli of Avatele often took his grandson Aokuso Pavihi to the Anzac preparations in the 1950s:

> I remember seeing tall men like Mitikoni of Mutalau, Taumatafiti of Liku, Talapoe of Tamakautoga and Sio Tagavili of Alofi doing their marching. It is a time for them to sing songs that they wrote themselves. I remember veterans Apelila from Tuapa, Liuvaie from Hakupu and Silimaka of Liku with his wife leading their comrades in singing.
>
> Most veterans wear their best white suits with medals on their left; I remember seeing only one or two wearing their war uniforms. You can hear the medals clicking as they march. After the parade my grandfather Taveli would take a sip of his Queen Anne whisky and take a smoke from his pipe … My grandfather was a pastor and I thought he won't take alcohol, but he told me that it is the only time he surrendered his pastoral duties and put on his hat as a returned serviceman.[26]

Each year the commemorations followed a similar pattern, with variations to allow for the weather or the need to load a freight vessel – and for the increasing age of the veterans. The Dawn Parade always centred on the memorial on the Alofi green and the morning church service was held in the Alofi church. Morning tea was held in various locations, including the home of Percy Walsh in Alofi South and the New Zealand Residence at Tapeu. When Poppy Day was introduced in 1968, the funds raised helped support elderly ex-servicemen and war widows.[27]

16/1055 Private Ikitaue of Hakupu has a locally made headstone that shows he was 'a returned soldier and a shopman'. He also has an official headstone in front but it has not lasted as well. AUTHOR'S COLLECTION

Percy Walsh worked with Sitemi Luisi of Hakupu, who had served in World War II, to gain war pensions for the 63 members of the Niue contingent still living in 1946. Doctors went to Niue to assess the men but this was difficult because there were no thorough medical records from the time of enlistment and the time of discharge. The extremely cursory medical examinations on enlistment, compounded as they were by language problems, made it difficult to assess the part that the men's war service had played in their current state of health. Some men mistook the purpose of the review of their health in 1946 and tried to hide any health issues, in the hope they could once again serve in the army.[28] There was some discussion as to whether the men from the Niue contingent should receive anything, given the nature of their involvement. 'Some people said that we were not heroes as we did not actually fight … Some said that we received a war pension for nothing. Those people did not think properly, that [we went] through the training, sickness and many hardships … trying to win the war.'[29]

There are a small number of official headstones on Niue such as this one for 16/1038 Private Faletogia of Mutalau. AUTHOR'S COLLECTION

Some of the men on the island did eventually receive a war pension, and others were successful in obtaining one in later life after they moved to New Zealand. They may, however, have been unhappy with the amount as this was tied directly to a medical estimate of the degree of incapacity attributable to war service and, in this regard, illness was more difficult to assess than injury. There was also the question of the Niuean men's eligibility for official headstones on war graves – the graves of soldiers who had died while serving or who died subsequently as a result of their war service. When the question of official headstones was raised in 1921 the resident commissioner, John Evison, explained to Internal Affairs, the department that had just been put in charge of war graves, that there were no cemeteries on the island, as people were buried on family land: for the 10 servicemen who had died since returning to the island, 'there were no permanent headstones on any of the graves but some were covered with coral and native lime'.[30] When the matter was again

Many villages have built their own memorial to commemorate their men; this one is in the village of Tamakautoga. AUTHOR'S COLLECTION

raised in 1929, the resident commissioner, Arthur Luckham, explained that a memorial had been erected on the Alofi green. 'I do not consider it necessary or advisable to take further action in the matter as I do not wish to interfere with the native custom.'[31] Nothing more was done until 1953 when the policy of supplying official headstones for those who qualified was again raised with the War Graves Division of Internal Affairs. By this time some families had imported headstones from New Zealand, but they were the exception as few could afford the cost. Some families managed to secure an official headstone for an ex-serviceman who had died, but these are still a rarity on the island.[32]

In recent times, the families of the servicemen have come together to remember their men on Anzac Day. There are memorials in many of the villages and, as in New Zealand, Anzac Day commemorations have grown

War memorial in the village of Mutalau. AUTHOR'S COLLECTION

in importance. Niuean communities in New Zealand and in Australia now hold their own Anzac Day services, too, and some have erected memorials – such as in Mt Roskill War Memorial Park in Auckland, and in Brisbane. The premier of Niue, the Honourable Toke Talagi, was granted an audience with Queen Elizabeth II in October 2015; he quoted to her the words sent to her grandfather King George V in 1914: 'I am the island of Niue, a small child that stands up to help.' The premier also visited Hornchurch, where he took part in a church service and thanked the people for the kindness they had shown to the Niue men back in 1916. When a group from the Niue RSA visited Hornchurch in 2016 they presented a commemorative plaque to mark the link between Hornchurch and Niue: it has been installed in St Andrew's Church, the scene of four Niuean funerals during the Great War.

Centenary commemorations in New Zealand and in Niue have heightened awareness of the involvement of the men from Niue. Their contribution, like that of the Cook Islands, is now more prominently recognised at Anzac events in New Zealand and in media coverage of the commemorations. Niue has now had 43 years of self-government in free association with New Zealand but the shared experience of the Great War remains as a strong bond between the two countries.

For some on Niue it must have been difficult to understand why these men ever went to a war on the other side of the world in the first place. As Niuean writer John Pule expresses it, through the words of his matriarch, Atalagi:

> Old people like herself had heard of New Zealand so much especially the two great wars. She lost a brother in the first and she never really understood why a close-blood could go away from his home and fanau, where his pito is buried, where his people call his name, how he could leave and fight and be ready to throw away his mana to die for someone else's cause without really knowing the stranger's name.[33]

For the men who made that journey, however, their pride was real, and that pride has been handed down to succeeding generations. As one serviceman expressed it, 'I will never forget that I am Private Puleoti Peni, No. 16/1111, New Zealand Expeditionary Force, Alofi Tokelau, Niue Island.'[34]

The plaque presented by the New Zealand government in October 2015 to mark the centenary of the departure for war of the Niue contingent. It is situated above the wharf, where families gathered in 1915 to watch their men depart. AUTHOR'S COLLECTION

Afterword

Alofi, 13 October 2015. Niuean families have been gathering from around the island since mid-morning. They come into the main village in cars, on motorbikes and on the back of trucks. They are wearing their Sunday best and they have their baskets of umu kai to add to the feast that will take place later. Preparations have been underway for several days to erect coconut-palm shelters around the church and on the village green. The final touches have been made to the new memorials to be unveiled in the afternoon.

The airport is busy. The Royal New Zealand Air Force arrives with the official party from the New Zealand government and a group from the New Zealand Armed Forces. These are young men and women from all branches of the services and all of Niuean descent. They wear their uniforms proudly and, for most, it is the first time they have set foot on Niue. Next to arrive is the Air New Zealand flight bringing Niuean families home. Others arrived on a flight several days earlier and they have been reconnecting with family who still live on Niue. There are family groups consisting of several generations, the younger ones bringing the matua, the elders, home. They are greeted at the airport by family and village members. Kahoa, necklaces of flowers and leaves, are placed around their necks. For many of these people, like the servicemen and women, it is their first visit to Niue. They have all come for one purpose: to give thanks to their men who sailed from Niue exactly 100 years ago to make their contribution to the Great War.

The service is held in the church at Alofi, just as it was 100 years ago. The earlier church building has long since been wrecked in a cyclone but the new church stands on the same site. From inside, it is possible to look out to Alofi Bay where once the *Te Anau* lay waiting to load the troops. The New Zealand officials are at the front of the church, as they were 100 years ago, but now they are the guests of the Niue government and the premier. The story of the

Niueans' journey to war and back is recounted in small excerpts, alternating Vagahau Niue and English; all the participants are direct descendants of men from the Niue contingent. There are hymns in Vagahau Niue, some with the whole congregation, some performed by particular villages. There is a sermon. And just as the church overflowed in October 1915, so it overflows today and many sit quietly out on the Alofi green.

The church service is followed by a ceremony at the lookout above the wharf. Families crowded here in 1915 to watch their men leave for war. Now they watch as a new memorial and plaque are unveiled and a storyboard is revealed that will tell visitors to the island of this defining moment in Niuean history. The servicemen and women from the New Zealand Forces appear from behind and present a haka, a Māori challenge, to those assembled before the memorial. As the official party now moves across the road to the village green and the official Niue war memorial, a party of Niuean warriors appear and perform a takalo, a Niuean challenge. There are speeches, prayers and the unveiling of a new memorial built by the Niue Returned Services Association.

Then the time comes for the laying of wreaths. They were made in the villages overnight as families sat together sharing their stories of the past. They have been made with local flowers and leaves and vines, and they have been woven with love. Some have a photograph attached. And as the families come forward in their groups to the memorial, the younger ones helping their elders, the most moving part of the proceedings has been reached. Some families carry a framed photo of their man. Some are wearing a photo around their neck. As they stand before the memorial they are weeping but they are filled with pride. There will be feasting in the evening, there will be laughter and singing and dancing, there will be stories told and retold, but right now, in front of the memorial, as they lay their wreaths, the people of Niue are remembering their men, they are reconnecting with their homeland and with their history.

Wreaths placed by families during the commemorations on 13 October 2015 lie at the base of the roll of honour on the village green in Alofi. AUTHOR'S COLLECTION

Appendices

APPENDIX 1
Men from Niue who served in the NZEF 1914–18

A. Men who served in the 3rd Maori Reinforcements

REG. NO.	NAME	RANK	NEXT OF KIN	VILLAGE
16/1030	Alotau	L/Cpl	Folole (W)	Alofi
16/1031	Apelila	Pte	Fehoko (W)	Tuapa
16/1032	Elone	Pte	Laka (F)	Hakupu
16/1035	Fakahoa	Pte	Pose (F)	Alofi
16/1041	Fakalagakai	Pte	Farani (F)	Lakepa
16/1040	Fakauka	Pte	Muitoa (F)	Lakepa
16/1037	Falaile	Pte	Tamahemata (W)	Mutalau
16/1044	Falaoa	Pte	Tosene (F)	Avatele
16/1038	Faletogia	Pte	Uesi (F)	Mutalau
16/1036	Fanatoa	Pte	Mago (F)	Tamakautoga
16/1043	Fanavai	Pte	Mareni (F)	Lakepa
16/1034	Fasene	Cpl	Tosene (F)	Avatele
16/1348	Fata	Pte	Line (M)	Tuapa
16/1042	Fatamaka	Pte	Taufitimoka (W)	Lakepa
16/1039	Fati	Pte	Togia (F)	Mutalau
16/1046	Filitoua	Pte	Felevehetupe (W)	Makefu
16/1047	Finiki	Pte	Tavita (F)	Alofi
16/1045	Fohetaha	Pte	Liliola (W)	Alofi
16/1048	Gumaka	Pte	Tifaogo (W)	Hikutavake
16/1049	Gutupulega	Pte	Tagaloa (M)	Mutalau
16/1371	Harry, Purie Davi	Pte	Nuitoga (F)	Liku
16/1051	Hegatuki	Pte	Mele (W)	Alofi
16/1052	Hemu	Sgt	Tifuonga (S)	Hikutavake
16/1050	Heti	Pte	Tio (F)	Tamakautoga
16/1053	Hipa	Cpl	Tifa (W)	Hikutavake
16/1056	Ikihega	Pte	Hulu (W)	Mutalau
16/1055	Ikitaue	Pte	Kalopa (F)	Hakupu
16/1057	Ikito	Pte	Ikinei (F)	Tuapa

REG. NO.	NAME	RANK	NEXT OF KIN	VILLAGE
16/1054	Imiu	Pte	Felolini (W)	Hakupu
16/1062	Kaimanu	Pte	Tapufa (W)	Hikutavake
16/1059	Kamupeli	Pte	Ahitau (W)	Hakupu
16/1063	Kanatau	Pte	Leone (W)	Makefu
16/1058	Ku	Pte	Totule (F)	Tamakautoga
16/1060	Kuluia	Pte	Finele (W)	Alofi
16/1061	Kulupa	Pte	Patoga (F)	Hikutavake
16/1080	Lagigie	Pte	Taneti (W)	Tuapa
16/1064	Lapa	Cpl	Tegiafulu (F)	Tamakautoga
16/1081	Latitu	Pte	Fakaaga (M)	Tuapa
16/1066	Latoa	Pte	Finiata (W)	Hakupu
16/1068	Latoa	Cpl	Ikinofo (F)	Alofi
16/1077	Laufoli	Pte	Peau (B)	Liku
16/1349	Lauho	Pte	Lueua (M)	Lakepa
16/1082	Laupa	Pte	Fakalaga (F)	Makefu
16/1084	Lautagata	Pte	Nia (F)	Makefu
16/1071	Lavaika	Pte	Tavita (F)	Alofi
16/1072	Lavini	Pte	Taufitimoka (W)	Hikutavake
16/1070	Leini	Pte	Latika (F)	Alofi
16/1074	Leotoga	Pte	Pakitoa (F)	Hikutavake
16/1078	Levi	Pte	Taleula (F)	Avatele
16/1076	Likatau	Pte	Taumanogi (M)	Alofi
16/1079	Litioti	Pte	Tomumu (F)	Avatele
16/1073	Litipa	Pte	Puhetoa (W)	Hikutavake
16/1083	Liu	Pte	Togialele (F)	Tuapa
16/1065	Liuvaie	Pte	Ilai (F)	Hakupu
16/1069	Lui	Pte	Tiahi (W)	Alofi
16/1067	Luki	Pte	Lagilela (F)	Hakupu
16/1075	Lukupa	Pte	Lino (W)	Liku
16/1086	Maka	Pte	Motutoa (F)	Hakupu
16/1094	Makafitu	Pte	Vavahe (F)	Mutalau
16/1092	Malefitu	Pte	Tumuaki (W)	Alofi
16/1102	Manatoa	Cpl	Muahemotu (W)	Tuapa
16/1093	Manu	Pte	Tiale (W)	Liku
16/1090	Manuela	L/Cpl	Nofoagahemata (W)	Alofi
16/1101	Matiutama	Pte	Matiu (F)	Makefu
16/1085	Meti	Pte	Ukufia (F)	Tamakautoga
16/1100	Mitihepi	Pte	Lamatoa (F)	Makefu
16/1087	Mitikele	Pte	Hegatagaloa (W)	Hakupu

REG. NO.	NAME	RANK	NEXT OF KIN	VILLAGE
16/1097	Mitikoni	Pte	Togiatau (F)	Mutalau
16/1095	Mitikoneua	Pte	Kalaina (M)	Mutalau
16/1099	Mitiloti	Pte	Mititola (F)	Avatele
16/1096	Mitipauni	Pte	Tamatagi (F)	Mutalau
16/1089	Moana	L/Cpl	Mata (M)	Alofi
16/1088	Moki	Pte	Pokihega (F)	Fatiau
16/1103	Motutoa	Pte	Fahisifa (F)	Tuapa
16/1098	Muimatagi	Pte	Hega (M)	Mutalau
16/1105	None	Pte	Manamana (F)	Avatele
16/1104	Nui, Alec	Cpl	Ligimata (W)	Alofi
16/1106	Otitoa	Pte	Tuleikafa (W)	Hakupu
16/1112	Pafalani	Pte	Pulegapule (F)	Hikutavake
16/1307	Pauhumoana	Pte	Nuitoga (F)	Liku
16/1119	Pakitau	Pte	Pepe (W)	Mutalau
16/1123	Paleko	Pte	Lafu (F)	Makefu
16/1125	Patuki	Pte	Fakato (M)	Alofi
16/1128	Peki	Pte	Tapola (W)	Alofi
16/1116	Peneholo	Pte	Foufou (W)	Liku
16/1115	Peni	Pte	Puakafa (W)	Hikutavake
16/1122	Pieti	Pte	Tifaua (W)	Lakepa
16/1118	Pimeleko	Pte	Matafetu (W)	Mutalau
16/1126	Pineki	Pte	Lakaheone (W)	Alofi
16/1110	Pinimaka	Pte	Mugaiki (F)	Alofi
16/1114	Pita	Pte	Malamatagaloa (W)	Hikutavake
16/1117	Poihalagi	Pte	Kalika (B)	Liku
16/1108	Poimatagi	Pte	Tiupeli (W)	Hakupu
16/1120	Puhotau	Pte	Togiatau (F)	Mutalau
16/1113	Pulegamotu	Pte	Kilipula (F)	Hakupu
16/1124	Pulegatau	Pte	Puletekai (F)	Tuapa
16/1127	Pulekanamata	Pte	Maea (M)	Makefu
16/1121	Pulemoana	Pte	Falani (F)	Lakepa
16/1111	Puleoti	Pte	Palego (W)	Alofi
16/1107	Pulu	Sgt	Vaiata (W)	Alofi
16/1109	Pulu	Pte	Limaole (W)	Tamakautoga
16/1130	Sisikefu	L/Cpl	Mohematagi (F)	Mutalau
16/1159	Tafale	Pte	Fiatagaloa (W)	Mutalau
16/1138	Tafana	Pte	Tagasili (F)	Hakupu
16/1147	Tafua	Pte	Tavaha (F)	Hikutavake
16/1166	Tagavaikuilu	Pte	Foufou (W)	Avatele

REG. NO.	NAME	RANK	NEXT OF KIN	VILLAGE
16/1143	Tagimau	L/Cpl	Niuloa (F)	Alofi
16/1168	Tahikona	Pte	Kapitiga (F)	Avatele
16/1162	Talauta	Pte	Alisi (W)	Mutalau
16/1132	Taleva	Pte	Filitupe (W)	Tamakautoga
16/1163	Tamahetoa	Pte	Mokapala (M)	Lakepa
16/1172	Tamapeau	Pte	Mokalagi (W)	Makefu
16/1154	Tamatafiti	Pte	Tupelima (W)	Liku
16/1155	Tauetuli	Pte	Hikiloto (W)	Liku
16/1173	Taufakavalu	Pte	Mataloa (M)	Tuapa
16/1136	Taukilo	Pte	Tolomaka (W)	Hakupu
16/1161	Taulisi	Pte	Faletiu (W)	Mutalau
16/1131	Tauliti	L/Cpl	Logatupe (W)	Tamakautoga
16/1165	Taumataua	Pte	Laka (M)	Lakepa
16/1167	Taveli	Pte	Hakeagaiki (F)	Avatele
16/1150	Tavili	Pte	Mokakolikoli (W)	Liku
16/1148	Tefatumoana	Cpl	Tetua (W)	Liku
16/1156	Tiafa	Pte	Matagaholo (W)	Mutalau
16/1178	Tilimaka	Pte	Patutoa (F)	Liku
16/1153	Tilo	Pte	Tialeone (W)	Liku
16/1134	Timoko	Pte	Kepuhega (F)	Hakupu
16/1141	Tio	Pte	Tulua (F)	Alofi
16/1142	Tionehafa	L/Cpl	Maina (W)	Alofi
16/1135	Tionemale	Pte	Mika (F)	Hakupu
16/1149	Tionemouga	Pte	Mokahulugia (W)	Liku
16/1133	Tionesini	Cpl	Manogimaife (W)	Hakupu
16/1137	Tionetali	Pte	Fanatau (F)	Hakupu
16/1146	Tionetini	Pte	Tuhau (F)	Tamakautoga
16/1129	Tipi	Pte	Punuatogia (F)	Mutalau
16/1164	Tiueatama	Pte	Luvea (F)	Lakepa
16/1091	Tiulai	Cpl	Hamoa (F)	Alofi
16/1169	Toamio	Pte	Foeume (F)	Avatele
16/1160	Togiaafu	Pte	Fenoga (W)	Mutalau
16/1157	Togiahemotu	Pte	Motu (F)	Mutalau
16/1170	Tohovaka	Pte	Palaone (F)	Makefu
16/1145	Toi	Pte	Lumeka (M)	Alofi
16/1158	Tomati	Pte	Nogihau (M)	Mutalau
16/1152	Tukimata	Pte	Talagi (F)	Liku
16/1144	Tukuaho	Pte	Tioti (F)	Alofi
16/1176	Uea	Sgt M	Tione Kilifi (B)	Alofi

REG. NO.	NAME	RANK	NEXT OF KIN	VILLAGE
16/1175	Uku	Pte	Alama (W)	Tuapa
16/1174	Ulukita	Pte	Fatu (F)	Lakepa
16/1179	Vaihola	Pte	Moleni (F)	Avatele
16/1180	Vaiua	Pte	Meleteine (M)	Avatele
16/1181	Vakatama	Pte	Tiahi (W)	Makefu
16/1177	Vasau	Pte	Siline (M)	Alofi
16/1178	Vilipate	Pte	Taufitione (W)	Liku

B. Men who served in other parts of the NZEF

REG. NO.	NAME	RANK	NEXT OF KIN	VILLAGE
12/1539	Alfred, William	Pte	Pilitasi (F)	Tuapa
3/1379	Allan, Make (Neki)	Pte	Toi (M)	Tamakautoga
38671	Cunningham, Ene	Pte	Fafili (W)	Mutalau
40542	Godsmark, A.G.	Pte	Ahome (W)	Avatele
20717	Haller, Mick (Patali)	Pte	John Haller (F)	Alofi
13/2202	Harrys, Jack	Pte	Robert Harrys (F)	Lakepa
12/2078	Paufai, Hono	Pte	Loine (M)	Niue

Next-of-kin are shown as: (F) Father, (M) Mother, (W) Wife, (B) Brother, (S) Sister

Compiled by the author from the Nominal Roll of the 3rd Maori Reinforcements, personnel files at New Zealand Archives, village memorials on Niue, the Niue Roll of Honour, and the list compiled by the Resident Commissioner's office on Niue in 1915.

APPENDIX 2

Shipping lists: Overseas movements of men from Niue who sailed with the 3rd Maori Reinforcements 1916

A. Men who sailed from Auckland to Egypt on SS *Navua*, 5 February 1916

REG. NO.	NAME	RANK	REG. NO.	NAME	RANK
16/1030	Alotau	L/Cpl	16/1081	Latitu	Pte
16/1032	Elone	Pte	16/1066	Latoa	Pte
16/1035	Fakahoa	Pte	16/1068	Latoa	Cpl
16/1041	Fakalagakai	Pte	16/1077	Laufoli	Pte
16/1040	Fakauka	Pte	16/1349	Lauho	Pte
16/1037	Falaile	Pte	16/1082	Laupa	Pte
16/1044	Falaoa	Pte	16/1084	Lautagata	Pte
16/1038	Faletogia	Pte	16/1071	Lavaika	Pte
16/1036	Fanatoa	Pte	16/1072	Lavini	Pte
16/1043	Fanavai	Pte	16/1070	Leini	Pte
16/1034	Fasene	Cpl	16/1074	Leotoga	Pte
16/1348	Fata	Pte	16/1076	Likatau	Pte
16/1042	Fatamaka	Pte	16/1079	Litioti	Pte
16/1039	Fati	Pte	16/1073	Litipa	Pte
16/1046	Filitoua	Pte	16/1083	Liu	Pte
16/1047	Finiki	Pte	16/1065	Liuvaie	Pte
16/1045	Fohetaha	Pte	16/1069	Lui	Pte
16/1048	Gumaka	Pte	16/1075	Lukupa	Pte
16/1049	Gutupulega	Pte	16/1086	Maka	Pte
16/1371	Harry, PD	Pte	16/1094	Makafitu	Pte
16/1051	Hegatuki	Pte	16/1092	Malefitu	Pte
16/1052	Hemu	Sgt	16/1102	Manatoa	Cpl
16/1053	Hipa	Cpl	16/1090	Manuela	L/Cpl
16/1055	Ikitaue	Pte	16/1101	Matiutama	Pte
16/1057	Ikito	Pte	16/1085	Meti	Pte
16/1054	Imiu	Pte	16/1100	Mitihepi	Pte
16/1062	Kaimanu	Pte	16/1087	Mitikele	Pte
16/1059	Kamupeli	Pte	16/1097	Mitikoni	Pte
16/1063	Kanatau	Pte	16/1095	Mitikoneua	Pte
16/1058	Ku	Pte	16/1099	Mitiloti	Pte
16/1060	Kuluia	Pte	16/1096	Mitipauni	Pte
16/1061	Kulupa	Pte	16/1089	Moana	L/Cpl
16/1080	Lagigie	Pte	16/1088	Moki	Pte
16/1064	Lapa	Pte	16/1103	Motutoa	Pte

REG. NO.	NAME	RANK	REG. NO.	NAME	RANK
16/1098	Muimatagi	Pte	16/1161	Taulisi	Pte
16/1105	None	Pte	16/1131	Tauliti	L/Cpl
16/1104	Nui, Alec	Cpl	16/1165	Taumataua	Pte
16/1106	Otitoa	Pte	16/1167	Taveli	Pte
16/1112	Pafalani	Pte	16/1150	Tavili	Pte
16/1307	Pauhumoana	Pte	16/1148	Tefatumoana	Cpl
16/1119	Pakitau	Pte	16/1156	Tiafa	Pte
16/1123	Paleko	Pte	16/1178	Tilimaka	Pte
16/1125	Patuki	Pte	16/1153	Tilo	Pte
16/1115	Peni	Pte	16/1134	Timoko	Pte
16/1122	Pieti	Pte	16/1141	Tio	Pte
16/1118	Pimeleko	Pte	16/1142	Tionehafa	L/Cpl
16/1126	Pineki	Pte	16/1135	Tionemale	Pte
16/1110	Pinimaka	Pte	16/1149	Tionemouga	Pte
16/1114	Pita	Pte	16/1133	Tionesini	Cpl
16/1117	Poihalagi	Pte	16/1137	Tionetali	Pte
16/1108	Poimatagi	Pte	16/1146	Tionetini	Pte
16/1120	Puhotau	Pte	16/1129	Tipi	Pte
16/1113	Pulegamotu	Pte	16/1164	Tiueatama	Pte
16/1124	Pulegatau	Pte	16/1091	Tiulai	Cpl
16/1127	Pulekanamata	Pte	16/1169	Toamio	Pte
16/1121	Pulemoana	Pte	16/1157	Togiahemotu	Pte
16/1111	Puleoti	Pte	16/1170	Tohovaka	Pte
16/1107	Pulu	Sgt	16/1145	Toi	Pte
16/1109	Pulu	Pte	16/1158	Tomati	Pte
16/1130	Sisikefu	L/Cpl	16/1152	Tukimata	Pte
16/1159	Tafale	Pte	16/1144	Tukuaho	Pte
16/1138	Tafana	Pte	16/1176	Uea	Sgt M
16/1147	Tafua	Pte	16/1175	Uku	Pte
16/1166	Tagavaikuila	Pte	16/1174	Ulukita	Pte
16/1143	Tagimau	L/Cpl	16/1179	Vaihola	Pte
16/1168	Tahikona	Pte	16/1180	Vaiua	Pte
16/1162	Talauta	Pte	16/1181	Vakatama	Pte
16/1132	Taleva	Pte	16/1177	Vasau	Pte
16/1163	Tamahetoa	Pte			
16/1154	Tamatafiti	Pte			
16/1155	Tauetuli	Pte			
16/1136	Taukilo	Pte			

B. Men invalided home from Egypt

From Suez on HT *Tahiti*, 5 May 1916

REG. NO.	NAME	RANK
16/1034	Fasene	Cpl
16/1070	Leine	Pte
16/1092	Malefitu	Pte
16/1101	Matiutama	Pte
16/1096	Mitipauni	Pte
16/1307	Pauhumoana	Pte
16/1127	Pulekanamata	Pte
16/1161	Taulisi	Pte
16/1131	Tauliti	L/Cpl
16/1141	Tio	Pte
16/1137	Tionetali	Pte
16/1144	Tukuaho	Pte

From Suez on SS *Maunganui*, 7 May 1916

REG. NO.	NAME	RANK
16/1122	Pieti	Pte
16/1174	Ulukita	Pte

From Suez on HT *Ulimaroa*, 11 June 1916

REG. NO.	NAME	RANK
16/1036	Fanatoa	Pte
16/1055	Ikitaue	Pte
16/1061	Kulupa	Pte
16/1095	Mitikoneua	Pte
16/1103	Motutoa	Pte
16/1098	Muimatagi	Pte
16/1120	Puhotau	Pte
16/1121	Pulemoana	Pte
16/1163	Tamahetoa	Pte

From Suez on SS *Navua*, 26 June 1916

REG. NO.	NAME	RANK
16/1079	Litioti	Pte

C. Men who sailed from Egypt to France

From Port Said to Marseilles on SS *Canada*, 9 April 1916

REG. NO.	NAME	RANK
16/1035	Fakahoa	Pte
16/1040	Fakauka	Pte
16/1037	Falaile	Pte
16/1044	Falaoa	Pte
16/1038	Faletogia	Pte
16/1046	Filitoua	Pte
16/1045	Fohetaha	Pte
16/1048	Gumaka	Pte
16/1371	Harry, PD	Pte
16/1052	Hemu	L/Cpl
16/1053	Hipa	Cpl
16/1063	Kanatau	Pte
16/1058	Ku	Pte
16/1080	Lagigie	Pte
16/1064	Lapa	Pte
16/1081	Latitu	Pte
16/1066	Latoa	Pte
16/1068	Latoa	Cpl
16/1349	Lauho	Pte
16/1082	Laupa	Pte
16/1084	Lautagata	Pte
16/1071	Lavaika	Pte
16/1072	Lavini	Pte
16/1069	Lui	Pte
16/1102	Manatoa	Cpl
16/1099	Mitiloti	Pte
16/1104	Nui, Alec	Cpl
16/1119	Pakitau	Pte
16/1123	Paleko	Pte
16/1125	Patuki	Pte
16/1118	Pimeleko	Pte
16/1110	Pinimaka	Pte
16/1117	Poihalagi	Pte
16/1108	Poimatagi	Pte
16/1111	Puleoti	Pte
16/1107	Pulu	Sgt
16/1109	Pulu	Pte
16/1130	Sisikefu	L/Cpl
16/1159	Tafale	Pte
16/1143	Tagimau	L/Cpl
16/1162	Talauta	L/Cpl
16/1132	Taleva	Pte
16/1154	Tamatafiti	Pte
16/1155	Tauetuli	Pte
16/1136	Taukilo	Pte
16/1167	Taveli	Pte
16/1150	Tavili	Pte
16/1148	Tefatumoana	Cpl
16/1156	Tiafa	Pte
16/1153	Tilo	Pte
16/1134	Timoko	Pte
16/1142	Tionehafa	L/Cpl
16/1135	Tionemale	Pte
16/1149	Tionemouga	Pte
16/1133	Tionesini	Cpl
16/1146	Tionetini	Pte
16/1169	Toamio	Pte
16/1158	Tomati	Pte
16/1180	Vaiua	Pte
16/1177	Vasau	Pte

From Alexandria to Marseilles on SS *Ivernia*, 20 May 1916

REG. NO.	NAME	RANK	REG. NO.	NAME	RANK
16/1032	Elone	Pte	16/1106	Otitoa	Pte
16/1041	Fakalagakai	Pte	16/1112	Pafalani	Pte
16/1043	Fanavai	Pte	16/1115	Peni	Pte
16/1348	Fata	Pte	16/1126	Pineki	Pte
16/1042	Fatamaka	Pte	16/1114	Pita	Pte
16/1039	Fati	Pte	16/1113	Pulegamotu	Pte
16/1047	Finiki	Pte	16/1124	Pulegatau	Pte
16/1049	Gutupulega	Pte	16/1138	Tafana	Pte
16/1051	Hegatuki	Pte	16/1147	Tafua	Pte
16/1057	Ikito	Pte	16/1166	Tagavaikuila	Pte
16/1054	Imiu	Pte	16/1168	Tahikona	Pte
16/1059	Kamupeli	Pte	16/1165	Taumataua	Pte
16/1060	Kuluia	Pte	16/1178	Tilimaka	Pte
16/1077	Laufoli	Pte	16/1129	Tipi	Pte
16/1074	Leotoga	Pte	16/1164	Tiueatama	Pte
16/1076	Likatau	Pte	16/1091	Tiulai	Cpl
16/1073	Litipa	Pte	16/1157	Togiahemotu	Pte
16/1083	Liu	Pte	16/1170	Tohovaka	Pte
16/1065	Liuvaie	Pte	16/1145	Toi	Pte
16/1075	Lukupa	Pte	16/1152	Tukimata	Pte
16/1086	Maka	Pte	16/1176	Uea	Sgt M
16/1090	Manuela	L/Cpl	16/1175	Uku	Pte
16/1085	Meti	Pte	16/1179	Vaihola	Pte
16/1100	Mitihepi	Pte	16/1181	Vakatama	Pte
16/1097	Mitikoni	Pte			
16/1089	Moana	L/Cpl			
16/1088	Moki	Pte			
16/1105	None	Pte			

From Alexandria to Marseilles on SS *Ivernia*, 26 July 1916

REG. NO.	NAME	RANK	REG. NO.	NAME	RANK
16/1030	Alotau	L/Cpl	16/1094	Makafitu	Pte

D. Men who sailed from England to New Zealand

On HT *Corinthic*, 17 June 1916

REG. NO.	NAME	RANK	REG. NO.	NAME	RANK
16/1041	Fakalagakai	Pte	16/1110	Pinimaka	Pte
16/1040	Fakauka	Pte	16/1124	Pulegatau	Pte
16/1037	Falaile	Pte	*16/1107	Pulu	Sgt
16/1043	Fanavai	Pte	16/1138	Tafana	Pte
16/1348	Fata	Pte	16/1165	Taumataua	Pte
16/1042	Fatamaka	Pte	16/1156	Tiafa	Pte
16/1048	Gumaka	Pte	16/1178	Tilimaka	Pte
16/1049	Gutupulega	Pte	16/1153	Tilo	Pte
16/1057	Ikito	Pte	16/1142	Tionehafa	L/Cpl
16/1059	Kamupeli	Pte	16/1146	Tionetini	Pte
16/1080	Lagigie	Pte	16/1129	Tipi	Pte
16/1068	Latoa	Cpl	*16/1164	Tiueatama	Pte
16/1077	Laufoli	Pte	16/1091	Tiulai	Cpl
16/1349	Lauho	Pte	16/1157	Togiahemotu	Pte
16/1074	Leotoga	Pte	16/1170	Tohovaka	Pte
16/1076	Likatau	Pte	16/1158	Tomati	Pte
16/1069	Lui	Pte	16/1176	Uea	Sgt M
16/1089	Moana	L/Cpl	*16/1179	Vaihola	Pte
16/1105	None	Pte			
16/1125	Patuki	Pte			
*16/1115	Peni	Pte			
*16/1126	Pineki	Pte			

* Died at sea

On SS *Arawa*, 14 July 1916

REG. NO.	NAME	RANK	REG. NO.	NAME	RANK
16/1032	Elone	Pte	16/1081	Latiu	Pte
16/1035	Fakahoa	Pte	16/1082	Laupa	Pte
16/1038	Faletogia	Pte	16/1084	Lautagata	Pte
16/1039	Fati	Pte	16/1072	Lavini	Pte
16/1045	Fohetaha	Pte	16/1073	Litipa	Pte
16/1371	Harry, PD	Pte	16/1083	Liu	Pte
16/1052	Hemu	Sgt	16/1065	Liuvaie	Pte
16/1054	Imiu	Pte	16/1075	Lukupa	Pte
16/1058	Ku	Pte	16/1086	Maka	Pte
16/1060	Kuluia	Pte	16/1102	Manatoa	Cpl
16/1064	Lapa	Cpl	16/1090	Manuela	L/Cpl

REG. NO.	NAME	RANK	REG. NO.	NAME	RANK
16/1085	Meti	Pte	16/1147	Tafua	Pte
16/1100	Mitihepi	Pte	16/1166	Tagavaikuila	Pte
16/1097	Mitikoni	Pte	16/1143	Tagimau	L/Cpl
16/1099	Mitiloti	Pte	16/1168	Tahikona	Pte
16/1104	Nui, Alec	Cpl	16/1154	Tamatafiti	Pte
16/1106	Otitoa	Pte	16/1136	Taukilo	Pte
16/1112	Pafalani	Pte	16/1167	Taveli	Pte
16/1119	Pakitau	Pte	16/1150	Tavili	Pte
16/1123	Paleko	Pte	16/1134	Timoko	Pte
16/1118	Pimeleko	Pte	16/1135	Tionemale	Pte
16/1114	Pita	Pte	16/1169	Toamio	Pte
16/1117	Poihalagi	Pte	16/1145	Toi	Pte
16/1108	Poimatagi	Pte	16/1152	Tukimata	Pte
16/1113	Pulegamotu	Pte	16/1175	Uku	Pte
16/1111	Puleoti	Pte	16/1180	Vaiua	Pte
16/1109	Pulu	Pte	16/1181	Vakatama	Pte
16/1130	Sisikefu	L/Cpl			
16/1159	Tafale	Pte			

On SS *Willochra*, 12 August 1916

REG. NO.	NAME	RANK	REG. NO.	NAME	RANK
16/1063	Kanatau	Pte	16/1162	Talauta	L/Cpl

On HS *Marama*, 31 August 1916

REG. NO.	NAME	RANK	REG. NO.	NAME	RANK
16/1044	Falaoa	Pte	16/1053	Hipa	Cpl
16/1047	Finiki	Pte	16/1071	Lavaika	Pte
16/1051	Hegatuki	Pte	16/1149	Tionemouga	Pte

On SS *Rotorua*, 17 November 1916

REG. NO.	NAME	RANK	REG. NO.	NAME	RANK
16/1030	Alotau	L/Cpl	16/1094	Makafitu	Pte
16/1066	Latoa	Pte	16/1148	Tefatumoana	L/Cpl

Lists compiled by the author from information obtained from individual personnel files, New Zealand Archives

APPENDIX 3

Claims for separation allowances for wives and children of Niuean soldiers on active service

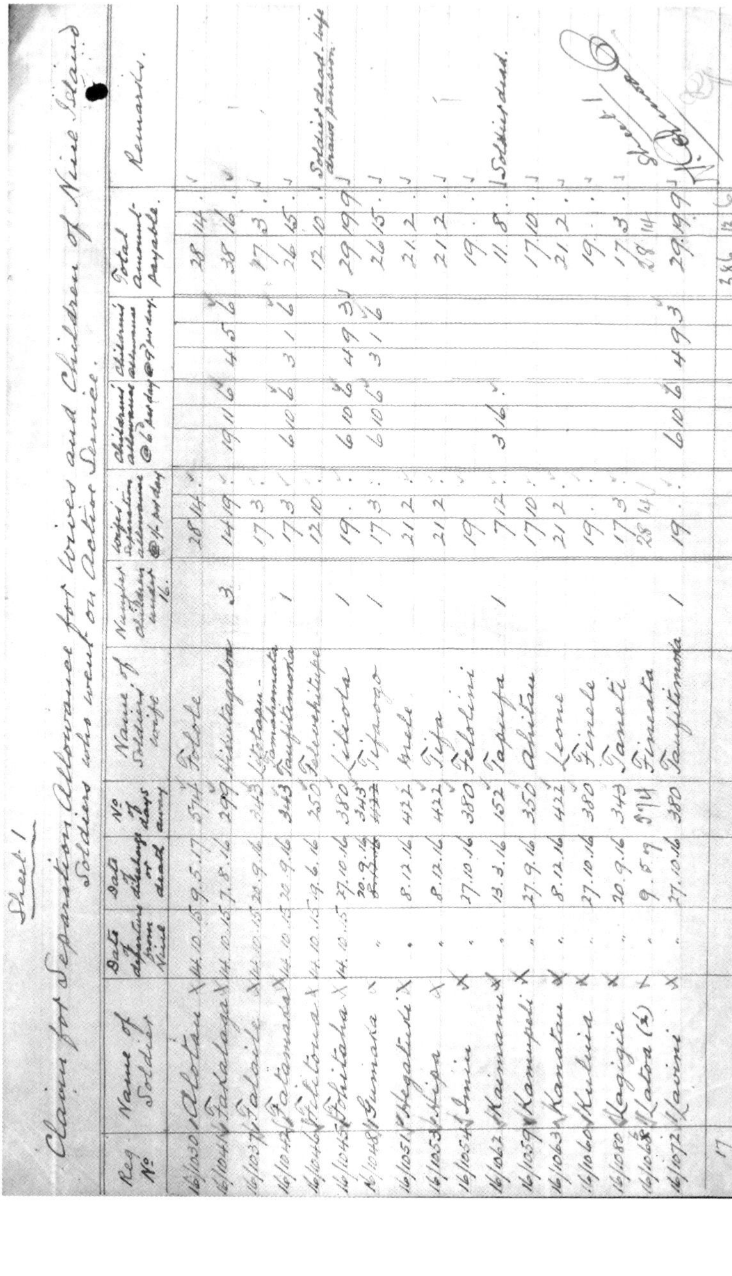

Sheet 1

Claim for Separation Allowance for Wives and Children of Niue Island Soldiers who went on Active Service.

Reg No	Name of Soldier	Date of departure from Niue	Date of discharge or death	No of days away	Name of Soldier's wife	Number children under 16	Wife's separation allowance @ 1/- per day	Children's allowance @ 6d per day	Children's allowance @ 9d per day	Total amount payable	Remarks
16/1030	Alotau	14.10.15	9.5.17	574	Folole		28 14 .			28 14 .	
16/1041	Fakalaga	14.10.15	7.8.16	299	Hikutagaloa	3	14 19 .	19 11 6	4 5 6	38 16 .	
16/1037	Falaile	14.10.15	20.9.16	343	Litotapu-Tamahomata		17 3 .			17 3 .	
16/1042	Fatamaka	14.10.15	20.9.16	343	Taufitimoka	1	17 3 .	6 10 6	3 1 6	26 15 .	
16/1046	Filitoua	14.10.15	9.6.16	250	Felevehitupe		12 10 .			12 10 .	Soldier dead. Wife draws pension
16/1045	Fohitaha	14.10.15	27.10.16	380	Liliola	1	19 . .	6 10 6	4 9 3	29 19 9	
16/1048	Gumaka	"	20.9.16	343	Tifaogo	1	17 3 .	6 10 6	3 1 6	26 15 .	
16/1051	Hegatiki	"	8.12.16	422	Mele		21 2 .			21 2 .	
16/1053	Hipa	"	8.12.16	422	Tifa		21 2 .			21 2 .	
16/1054	Imiu	"	27.10.16	380	Felolini		19 . .			19 . .	
16/1062	Kaimanu	"	13.3.16	152	Tapufa	1	7 12 .	3 16 .		11 8 .	Soldier dead.
16/1059	Kamupeli	"	27.9.16	350	Ahitau		17 10 .			17 10 .	
16/1063	Kanatau	"	8.12.16	422	Leone		21 2 .			21 2 .	
16/1060	Kuluia	"	27.10.16	380	Finele		19 . .			19 . .	
16/1080	Lagigie	"	20.9.16	343	Taneti		17 3 .			17 3 .	
16/1068	Latoa (2)	"	9.5.17	574	Fineata		28 14			28 14	
16/1072	Lavini	"	27.10.16	380	Taufitimoka	1	19 . .	6 10 6	4 9 3	29 19 9	
17										386 13 6	Sheet 1

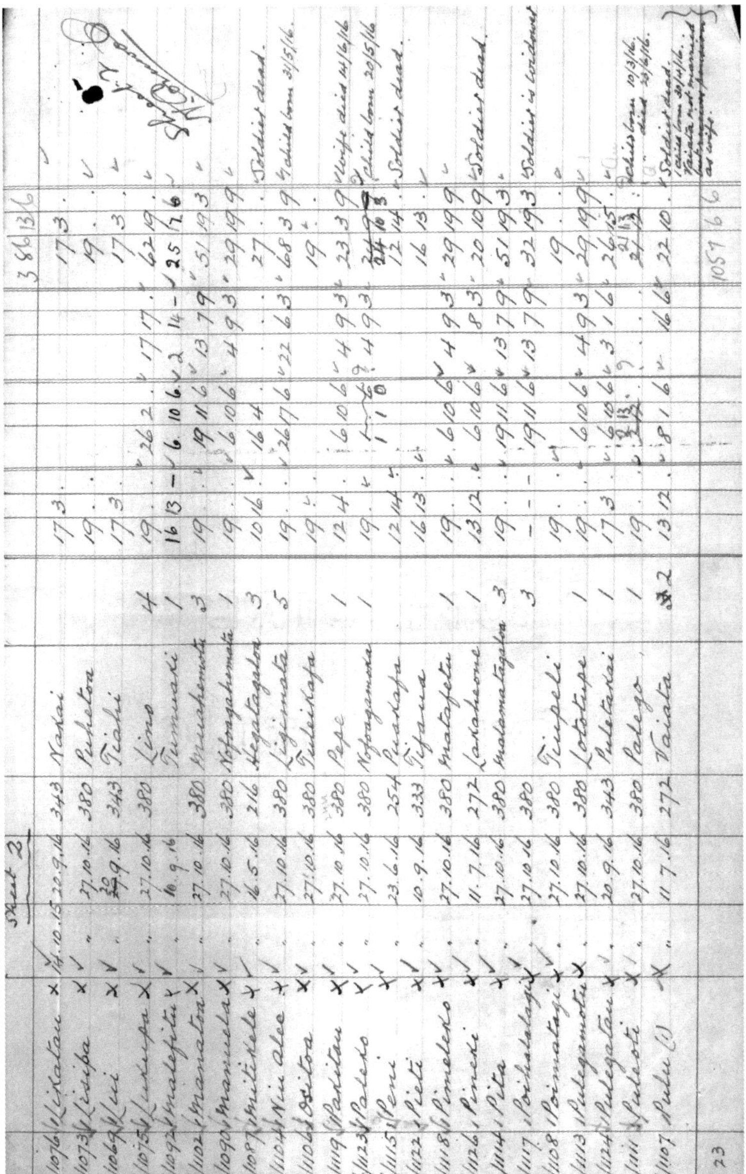

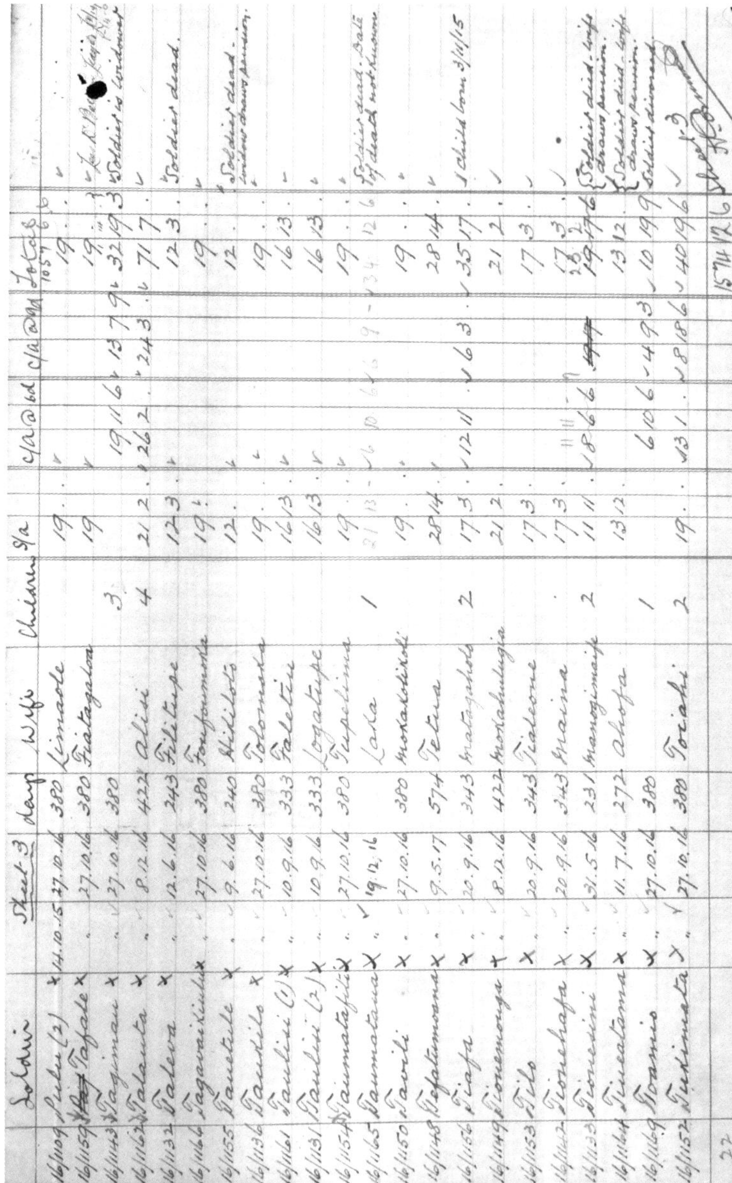

Sheet 3

	Soldier				days	Wife	Children	S/a	C/a @ 6d	C/a @ [illegible]	Totals	
16/1109	Pulu (2)	x	14.10.15	27.10.16	380	Limaole		19.			19.	
16/1159	Tafale	x		27.10.16	380	Fiatagaloa		19			19.	
16/1143	Tagimau	x		27.10.16	380		3		19 11 6	13 7 9	32 19 3	Soldier is widower
16/1163	Talauta	x		8.12.16	422	Alisi	4	21 2.	26 2.	24 3.	71 7.	
16/1132	Taleva	x		12.6.16	243	Filitupe		12 3.			12 3.	Soldier dead.
16/1166	Tagavaikiuku	x		27.10.16	380	Fonfoumole		19.			19.	
16/1155	Tautile	x		9.6.16	240	Hililoto		12.			12.	Soldier dead. widow draws pension.
16/1136	Taulilo	x		27.10.16	380	Tolomata		19.			19.	
16/1161	Taulisi (1)	x		10.9.16	333	Taletiu		16 13			16 13	
16/1131	Taulisi (2)	x		10.9.16	333	Logatupe		16 13			16 13	
16/1154	Taumatafiti	x		27.10.16	380	Tupelima		19.			19.	
16/1165	Taumatauaa	x		19.12.16		Lala	1	21 13	6 10	6 6 9	34 12 6	Soldier dead. Date of death not known
16/1150	Tavili	x		27.10.16	380	Mokakoliki		19.			19.	
16/1148	Tefatimoana	x		9.5.17	574	Tetua		28 14			28 14	
16/1156	Tiafa	x		20.9.16	343	Matagaholo	2	17 3	12 11	6 3	35 17	1 child born 3/11/15
16/1149	Tiomeouga	x		8.12.16	422	Mokahulugia		21 2			21 2	
16/1153	Tilo	x		20.9.16	343	Tialeone		17 3			17 3	
16/1142	Tionehafa	x		20.9.16	343	Maina		17 3			17 3	
16/1133	Tionisini	x		31.5.16	231	Manogimaifa	2	11 11	8 6 6		19 17 6	Soldier died, wife draws pension.
16/1164	Tiueatama	x		11.7.16	272	Ahofa		13 12			13 12	Soldier died, wife draws pension.
16/1169	Toamio	x		27.10.16	380		1		6 10 6	4 9 3	10 19 9	Soldier divorced
16/1152	Tukimata	x		27.10.16	380	Toiahi	2	19.	13 1.	8 18 6	40 19 6	
											1574 12 6	

22

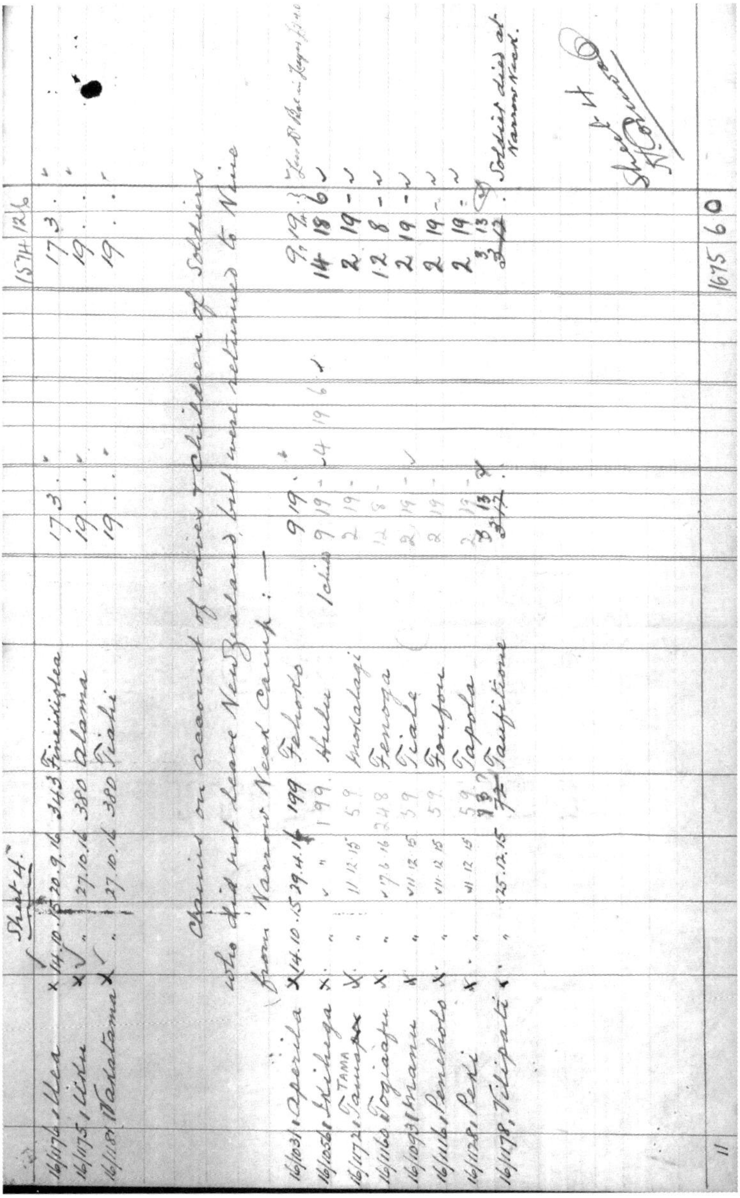
Sheet 4.

Claims on account of wives & children of soldiers who did not leave New Zealand but were returned to Niue from Narrow Neck Camp :—

Soldier died at Narrow Neck.

This appendix published with permission from Archives New Zealand, Department of Internal Affairs Te Tari Taiwhenua, AAYS 8638 844 31/419/15. Finance and Accounts-Pay and allowances-Niue Islanders.

Glossary

Vagahau Niue

Fale Fono – assembly house, parliament

fanau – birthplace

kahoa – necklace of flowers

malolō – strong, healthy

matua – elder

Pālagi – European

patuiki – monarch, king

Pelitānia – Britain

pito – umbilical cord

takalo – challenge

tāoga – treasure

tupuna – ancestor

umu kai – food cooked in an earth oven

vagahau – language

vaka – canoe, outrigger

Te Reo Māori

haka – fierce rhythmical dance, challenge

iwi – tribe

mana – prestige, power

marae – meeting place, local ceremonial centre

Pākehā – European

rangatira – chief or person of high rank

Notes

INTRODUCTION

1. Margaret Pointer, *Tagi Tote e Loto Haaku – My Heart Is Crying a Little: Niue Island involvement in the Great War 1914–1918*, trans. Kalaisi Folau (Suva: Institute of Pacific Studies and Government of Niue, 2000).
2. Santanu Das, 'Experiences of colonial troops', January 2014: bl.uk/world-war-one/articles/colonial-troops
3. Wilfred Owen, 'Strange meeting', found among his papers after Owen was killed in action, 4 November 1918.
4. See for example, Timothy Winegard, *Indigenous Peoples of the British Dominions and the First World War* (New York: Cambridge University Press, 2012).
5. Many of the medical assessment forms for Niuean men give one or other of these explanations for discharge from the NZ Army.
6. M. Sherwood, 'Racism by omission', *BBC History Magazine*, 29 December 2009: www.historyextra.com/contributions
7. The main omissions were on the brass plaque prepared in the 1970s to be placed outside the new Fale Fono: some Niuean names were missed, and names of some other Pacific Islanders appeared. The full list on the new National Memorial has corrected all these errors.
8. The population of Niue is now approximately 1500–1600, while in the 2013 New Zealand census 24,000 people identified as Niuean and nearly 80 per cent of these were born in New Zealand.
9. Margaret Pointer, 'Niue: Bringing the history home', in Katie Pickles et al. (eds), *History Making a Difference: New approaches from Aotearoa* (Newcastle upon Tyne, UK: Cambridge Scholars Publishing, 2017, 58–72).
10. Sifatagaloa Tulepu, who died only weeks before the 100th anniversary ceremonies in October 2015.

1. BACKGROUND TO WAR

1. Peter Adds in Sean Mallon, Kolokesa Māhina-Tuai & Damon Salesa (eds), *Tangata o le Moana: New Zealand and the people of the Pacific* (Wellington: Te Papa Press, 2012, 17).
2. Peter Crawford, *Nomads of the Wind: A natural history of Polynesia* (London: BBC Books, 1993).
3. Niall Ferguson, *Empire: How Britain made the modern world* (Penguin Books, London, 2003, 169).

4. Fataaiki to Sir G. Mitchell, WPHC, 3 November 1887, LMS Records relating to Niue Island 1861–1910, ATL Micro-MS-0471.
5. For more detail on New Zealand's role in Niue, see Margaret Pointer, *Niue 1774–1974: 200 years of contact and change* (Dunedin: Otago University Press, 2015).
6. The Pacific battle became known as the Battle of Coronel, and the Atlantic battle as the Battle of the Falkland Islands.
7. Over 300,000 Australians and nearly 100,000 New Zealanders were sent overseas during WWI; see awm.gov.au and nzhistory.govt.nz
8. See 'Pacific Islanders in the NZEF': nzhistory.govt.nz
9. Adrian Muckle, 'Kanak experiences of WWI: New Caledonia's tirailleurs and rebels', *History Compass*, vol. 6, no. 5, 2008, 1325–45.
10. See newspaper articles such as 'Tahitian native troops', *New Zealand Herald*, 25 April 1916, and 'Tirailleurs du Pacifique', *Dominion*, 1 July 1916.

2. PREPARATION FOR WAR

1. 'Lonely Pacific Islands', *Grey River Argus*, 4 September 1914.
2. 'Loyalty of Niue', *New Zealand Herald*, 6 October 1914.
3. Cullen to Lenwood, 4 October 1914, LMS records Niue 1910-53, ATL Micro-MS-Col-08-0701-1 (PMB 701).
4. Figures read out by Prime Minister Massey in parliament, 8 October 1914; see 'The Patriotic Fund', *Dominion*, 9 October 1914.
5. Ibid.
6. Ibid.
7. Cornwall to Pomare, 25 August 1915, ANZ AAYS 8638 AD1 9/219/1. Expeditionary Force-Rarotongans-Niue-Cook Islands.
8. *Western Daily Press*, 8 December 1914; *The Scotsman*, 16 December 1914; *Stonehaven Journal*, 17 December 1914.
9. 'The Patriotic Fund', *Dominion*, 9 October 1914.
10. See Ashley Jackson, 'The Empire at war', *BBC History Magazine*, vol. 9, no. 11, November 2008.
11. 'An astonished mariner', *Feilding Star*, 4 September 1914.
12. Cullen to Cornwall, 16 November 1914, LMS records Niue 1910-53, ATL Micro-MS-Col-08-0701-1 (PMB 701).
13. Latoa, Tagimau and Fakahoa. Recounted by 16/1068 Cpl Latoa. Transcript of interview on Radio Pacific on Anzac Day 1980. Kindly lent by Foufouhetogia Marion McQuoid QSM, granddaughter of Sgt Major Uea.
14. *Tohi Tala Niue* 49, 8 June 1984. Article on the death of Makapa Maka Folau (16/1086 Pte Maka), the last of the WWI veterans to pass away.
15. Recounted in the memoirs of 16/1111 Pte Puleoti, as retold by his son Vahatau. Family collection, Niue.

16. Holmes to Cornwall, 24 November 1914, LMS records Niue 1910-53, ATL Micro-MS-Col-08-0701-1 (PMB 701).
17. Cornwall to Cullen, 17 November 1914, ibid.
18. Holmes to Cornwall, 24 November 1914, ibid.
19. 'Military mysteries', *West Coast Times*, 28 February 1916.
20. Cullen to Lenwood, 30 January 1915, LMS records Niue 1910-53, ATL Micro-MS-Col-08-0701-1 (PMB 701).
21. Cullen to Mrs Beauchamp, 18 December 1915, ibid.
22. Deryck Scarr, *Ratu Sukuna: Soldier, statesman, man of two worlds* (London: Macmillan Education, 1980, 32).
23. *Press*, 6 August 1915.
24. The British dominions in 1914 were Australia, New Zealand, Canada, Newfoundland and South Africa.
25. Timothy Winegard, *Indigenous Peoples of the British Dominions and the First World War* (New York: Cambridge University Press, 2012, 68).
26. See P.S. O'Connor, 'The recruitment of Maori soldiers, 1914–1918', *Political Science,* vol. 19, 1967, 48–83.
27. Rekene Pehi Neho and 261 others. Petition handed to Lord Liverpool, governor-general, at Kaikohe in February 1916. ANZ ADBQ 16145 Allen1 3/ M1/57 3 Part 1. James Allen-Minister of Defence-ministerial files-correspondence with GG.
28. Pomare to Allen, 9 February 1915, ANZ AAYS 8638 AD1 9/219/1. Expeditionary Force-Rarotongans-Niue-Cook Islands.
29. Allen to Pomare, February 1915, ibid.
30. Allen to Pomare, 30 June 1915, ibid.
31. O'Connor, 'The recruitment of Maori soldiers', 60.

3. DEPARTURE FROM NIUE

1. 'The trip of the SS *John Williams*', *Samoanische Zeitung*, 16 October 1915.
2. Cullen to Foreign Secretary, LMS London, 20 December 1915, LMS Records Niue 1910-1953, ATL Micro-MS-Coll-08-0701-1.
3. See Margaret Pointer, *Niue 1774–1974: 200 years of contact and change* (Dunedin: Otago University Press, 2015, 182–92).
4. Territorial Force Carl Herman Seaforth [aka Carl Herman Schumacher], Captain, New Zealand Medical Corps, ANZ AABK 7291 W5614.
5. 'In far-off Niue: A happy island kingdom', *Ashburton Guardian*, 27 March 1916.
6. 'Call to the colours. Niue makes history', *New Zealand Herald*, 21 October 1915.
7. Transcript of interview with 16/1141 Private Tio, Niue Museum.
8. Department of Defence to Minister of Defence, 4 September 1915, ANZ AAYS 8638 AD1 9/219/Part 1. Expeditionary Force-Rarotongans-Niue-Cook Islands.

9. Cullen to Resident Commissioner, 5 January 1915, LMS Records Niue 1910-1953, ATL Micro-MS-Coll-08-0701-1.
10. Cullen to Foreign Secretary, LMS, 20 December 1915, ibid.
11. Cullen to Mrs Lawes, 23 October 1915, ibid.
12. R.H. Head to Cullen, 13 October 1915, ibid.
13. 'Call to the colours. Niue makes history', *New Zealand Herald*, 21 October 1915.
14. Cullen to Mrs Lawes, 23 October 1915, LMS Records Niue 1910-1953, ATL Micro-MS-Coll-08-0701-1.
15. The term 'Tommy' was used to refer to a private in the British Army. 'Fiapa' was the name Seaforth used for one of the Niuean men: it was probably his approximation of 16/1156 Tiafa (pronounced Siafa).
16. 'Call to the colours. Niue makes history', *New Zealand Herald*, 21 October 1915.
17. See Appendix 3: Claims for separation allowances for wives and children of Niue Island soldiers who went on active service.
18. Transcript of interviews with Tio and Tauliti in 1970s, Niue Museum.
19. *AJHR* 1917 A-3. Cornwall reports on destructive cyclone in January 1915 and subsequent drought.

4. TRAINING AT NARROW NECK

1. 'Recruits from Niue. Arrival of 150 natives', *New Zealand Herald*, 21 October 1915.
2. P.S. O'Connor, 'The recruitment of Maori soldiers, 1914–1918', *Political Science*, vol. 19, 1967, 50.
3. Pomare to Allen, 21 September 1915, ANZ AABK 18805 W5948 16/1330. Archibald MacDonald.
4. See *Dominion*, 5 September 1938, for an obituary of MacDonald. He served for the remainder of the war in the Auckland Regiment and after the war became collector of customs in Western Samoa.
5. 16/1309 George August Fromm, ANZ AABK Series 18805, NZ Defence Force Personnel Files.
6. 'Narrow Neck Camp: Commandant's inspection', *New Zealand Herald*, 23 October 1915.
7. 'Narrow Neck Camp: Maoris, Niue Islanders, and Rarotongans', *Otago Daily Times*, 9 November 1915.
8. 'Polynesian soldiers: Training camp scenes', *New Zealand Herald*, 30 October 1915.
9. 'Niueans' unpleasant day: Affected by the food', *Auckland Weekly News*, 4 November 1915.
10. 16/1141 Private Tio. Transcript of interview in 1970s, Niue Museum.
11. 'Polynesian soldiers. Training camp scenes', *New Zealand Herald*, 30 October 1915.
12. 'Maori Contingents: Reinforcements question', *Auckland Weekly News*, 25 November 1915.

13. Allen to Godley, 26 November 1915, ANZ ACID 25038 WA 252. Correspondence between General Sir Alexander Godley and Colonel Hon. Sir James Allen.
14. Cullen to Mrs Beauchamp, 18 December 1915, LMS records Niue 1910-53, ATL Micro-MS-Col-08-0701-1 (PMB 701).
15. These medical details have been extracted from individual personnel files but the identities have not been revealed: this policy was used throughout the work with medical records, in the interests of privacy.
16. *New Zealand Herald*, 28 December 1915.
17. 16/1371 Purie Davi Harry (Puleua) and 16/1307 Pauhumoana were the sons of Nuitoga of Liku.
18. *Auckland Star*, 22 January 1916, 4.
19. 'Polynesian soldiers: Training camp scenes', *New Zealand Herald*, 30 October 1915.
20. Damien Fenton, *New Zealand and the First World War 1914–1919* (Auckland: Penguin Books, 2013, 46–47).
21. 'Retailers' big fair: Fete at Narrow Neck', *Auckland Star*, 25 October 1915.
22. 'Military fete at Domain', *Auckland Star*, 25 November 1915.
23. 'Soldiers in camp: Yuletide at Narrow Neck', *New Zealand Herald*, 27 December 1915.
24. 'The training camps', *Auckland Star*, 28 December 1915.
25. 'Our Polynesian contingent', *Star*, editorial, 4 January 1916.
26. H.T.B. Drew (ed.), *The War Effort of New Zealand. Official History of New Zealand's Effort in the Great War*, vol. IV (Auckland: Whitcombe & Tombs, 1923).
27. Memoirs of 16/1111 Private Puleoti as retold by his son Vahatau. Personal collection, Niue.
28. 'Fine military spectacle', *New Zealand Herald*, 5 February 1916.
29. Biography of 16/1333 L/Cpl Kaipati, *Pacific Islanders in the NZEF*: nzhistory.govt.nz
30. Biography of the Leger brothers, *Pacific Islanders in the NZEF*: nzhistory.govt.nz

5. TO EGYPT

1. N. Boyack & J. Tolerton (eds), *In the Shadow of War* (Auckland: Penguin, 1990, 56).
2. 16/1141 Private Tio. Transcript of interview in 1970s, Niue Museum.
3. 16/1131 L/Cpl. Tauliti Talapoe. Transcript of interview in 1970s, Niue Museum.
4. In 1918, after the Armistice, the Suez War Memorial Cemetery was established and graves were transferred there from around the area. Kaimanu is one of 16 members of the NZEF who now lie in the Suez War Memorial Cemetery.
5. See Appendix 2 for shipping lists. Twenty-four men were sent back from Egypt in a number of different ships.
6. Randolph Norman Gray, Papers relating to WWI, ATL MS-Group-2302.
7. H. Stewart, *France. Official History of New Zealand's Effort in the Great War*, vol. II (Auckland: Whitcombe & Tombs, 1921, 9).

8. Chris Pugsley, *Te Hokowhitu a Tu: The Maori Battalion in the First World War* (Auckland: Reed, 1995, 45).
9. Eric Clarke, war diaries, 17 Nov. 1915–14 Dec. 1915, State Library NSW, Australia (Cairo, 17–31 March 1916).
10. Colin M. Gordon, 'Life of a Hospital Orderly in Cairo and England', ATL MS Papers 2514.
11. Colin Gordon in Boyack & Tolerton (eds), *In the Shadow of Wars*, 99.
12. Gen. Alexander Godley to Sir James Allen, 24 March 1916, ANZ ACID 25038 WA 252. Correspondence between General Sir Alexander Godley and Colonel Hon. Sir James Allen.
13. 16/1131 L/Cpl. Tauliti Talapoe. Transcript of interview in 1970s, Niue Museum.
14. Lord Plunket to Hon. James Allen, 6 April 1916, ANZ ACID 25038 WA 252, Item 3. Correspondence between General Sir Alexander Godley and Colonel Hon. Sir James Allen.
15. Sec. of State for Colonies to Governor of NZ, 23 January 1916, ANZ Register Official Correspondence Government House G22/13.23 Reference 273.
16. Dick Scott, *Would a Good Man Die? Niue Island, New Zealand and the late Mr Larsen* (Auckland: Hodder & Stoughton, 1993, 43).
17. Godley to Allen, 24 March 1916.
18. Clarke war diaries: Cairo, 17 April 1916.
19. Gray, Papers relating to WWI.
20. Wilfred Fitchett, 'The diaries of a front line soldier', unpublished, Auckland War Memorial Museum Library.
21. J. Cowan, *The Maoris in the Great War: A history of the New Zealand Native Contingent and the Pioneer Battalion. Official History of New Zealand's Effort in the Great War*, vol. III (Auckland: Whitcombe & Tombs, 1926, 74).
22. Gray, Papers relating to WWI.

6. IN FRANCE

1. Randolph Norman Gray, Papers relating to WWI, ATL MS-Group-2302.
2. H. Stewart, *France. Official History of New Zealand's Effort in the Great War*, vol. II (Auckland: Whitcombe & Tombs, 1921, 20).
3. Interview with Private (later Lieut. Col.) Lawrence Blyth, in N. Boyack & J. Tolerton (eds), *In the Shadow of War* (Auckland: Penguin Books, 1990, 57).
4. Stewart, *France*, 20.
5. Medical Officer, Pioneer Battalion, to NZ Division Headquarters, 20 April 1916, ANZ ACID WA97 3/item 4.
6. Gray, Papers relating to WWI.
7. Stewart, *France*, 21.

8. Gray, Papers relating to WWI.
9. Interview with Blyth, in Boyack & Tolerton, *In the Shadow of War*, 57.
10. NZ Maori Pioneer Battalion War Diary, 1-29 May 1916, ANZ ACID 18432 WA97.
11. Interview with Private Stan Stanfield, in Boyack & Tolerton, *In the Shadow of War*, 42.
12. See NZ Maori Pioneer Battalion war diaries online at Archives NZ for a daily summary of activities.
13. Correspondence between Allen and Godley, September–October 1916, ANZ ACID 25038 WA 252. Correspondence between General Sir Alexander Godley and Colonel Hon. Sir James Allen.
14. NZ Division Headquarters to Officer Commanding NZ Pioneer Battalion, 25 May 1916, ANZ ACID WA97 3/item 4.
15. Memoirs of 16/1111 Private Puleoti as retold by his son Vahatau. Personal collection, Niue.

7. HORNCHURCH, ENGLAND

1. Barbara Mannox, *Hornchurch and the New Zealand Connection* (London: Havering Library Service, 1993, 18–25).
2. C.T. Perfect, *Hornchurch During the Great War* (Colchester: Benham & Co., 1920, 242).
3. *AJHR* 1917 H-40, New Zealand War Contingent Association.
4. Ibid.
5. 'Women in industry and public life', *Auckland Star*, 4 October 1916.
6. 'Our Maori soldiers', *Waiapu Church Gazette*, 1 December 1915.
7. Ibid.
8. Sarah Lawes died in October 1917, aged 73. Frank Lawes died the following year, aged 74.
9. Sarah Lawes to James Cullen, 1 July 1916, LMS Records Niue 1910-1953, ATL Micro-MS-Coll-08-0701-1.
10. Information on Falaoa and Fasene from personal communication with Mele Vekula-Moonen, great-granddaughter, December 2016. See nzhistory.govt.nz/media/video/falaoa-and-niueans-great-war-story April 2017
11. Lawes to Cullen, 1 July 1916. Maggie is a daughter of Frank and Sarah Lawes, and Neville is their grandson.
12. LMS obituary to Mrs Lawes, October 1917. Copy held in personal papers of Lawes family and kindly lent by Jonathan Lawes, London, great-grandson of Frank and Sarah Lawes.
13. Ephesians VI, 'Therefore take up the whole armour of God …'
14. Lawes to Cullen, 1 July 1916.
15. Basil Thomson, *Savage Island. An account of a sojourn in Niue and Tonga* (London: John Murray, 1902), Preface.

16. Lawes to Cullen, 1 July 1916.
17. Perfect, *Hornchurch*, 242.
18. Ibid.
19. See Margaret Pointer, *Niue 1774–1974: 200 years of contact and change* (Dunedin: Otago University Press, 2015), chs 8 and 9 for discussion about and images of Togia.
20. Mannox, *Hornchurch and the New Zealand Connection*, 7.
21. Ibid.
22. Thomson, *Savage Island*.
23. Hon. Margaret Amherst, 'Niue', *Imperial Colonist*, 9 October 1916.
24. Ibid.

8. THE RETURN HOME

1. See Appendix 2 for shipping lists.
2. Writer and historian Dick Scott described the *Corinthic* as 'disease-ridden' in *Would a Good Man Die? Niue Island, New Zealand and the late Mr Larsen* (Auckland: Hodder & Stoughton, 1993, 43).
3. Interview by author with Gordon Maui Jackson, 21 April 1999, Niue.
4. Bert Stokes in N. Boyack & J. Tolerton (eds), *In the Shadow of War* (Auckland: Penguin Books, 1990, 225).
5. 'Niueans and New Zealanders entertained in Hobart', *The Mercury*, Hobart, Tasmania, 1 August 1916.
6. 'Niue gratitude: Testimonial to Captain Hart of the *Corinthic*', *Dominion*, 15 August 1916, 6.
7. 'Soldiers' homes', *New Zealand Herald*, 9 September 1915.
8. See chapter 10 for a photo of this visit.
9. NZEF London to Headquarters, Military Forces, Wellington, 16/1309 George August Fromm, Personnel file, ANZ AABK 18805 W5937.
10. Newspaper report, August 1916. In personal papers kindly lent by Mr Donald Fromm, son of George Fromm. The newspaper is not named.
11. 'Returning New Zealanders welcomed at Hobart', *Daily Post*, Hobart, 29 August 1916.
12. 'Back from the war', *New Zealand Herald*, 4 September 1916.
13. Godley to Allen, 8 September 1916, ANZ ACID 25038 WA 252. Correspondence between General Sir Alexander Godley and Colonel Hon. Sir James Allen.
14. Allen to Godley, 7 October 1916, ibid.
15. A.W. Robin to Minister of Defence, 7 August 1916, ANZ AAYS 8694 AD78. Discharged personnel-Niue Islanders and Rarotongans, general.
16. Ibid.
17. Ibid. Headquarters, Auckland Military District to Director of Base Records, Wellington, 24 June 1916.

18. Ibid.
19. Niue was fortunate that *Talune* did not normally call there, for this was the ship that carried the influenza epidemic to Samoa and other Pacific Islands in November 1918.
20. Interview with Corporal Latoa on Radio Pacific, Anzac Day 1980. Transcript kindly lent to author by Foufouhetogia Marion McQuoid QSM, granddaughter of Sergeant Major Uea.
21. Article on death of Mr Makapa Maka Folau, *Tohi Tala Niue*, vol. 49, no. 14, 8 June 1984.
22. Rev. Cullen to Rev. Horder, LMS Correspondence 28 September 1916, LMS Records Niue 1910-1953, ATL Micro-MS-Coll-08-0701-1.
23. *AJHR* 1919, vol. I, A-E A-3, 18.

9. OTHER NIUEANS WHO SERVED WITH NZEF

1. Resident Commissioner to Secretary, Cook Islands Dept. 26 March 1926, ANZ ACGA 8280 IT1, Niue-War medals, roll of honour, war graves.
2. Paufai was one of the first pupils at Tufukia school in 1909. When the teacher, George Malcolm, returned to New Zealand in 1911, Paufai accompanied him to continue his studies at his new school in the Hokianga. After Paufai's death in 1918, Malcolm placed a bereavement notice in the *New Zealand Herald* on behalf of Paufai's mother, Loine. See Lisa Truttman, 'To serve and die so far away from home', *NZ Legacy,* 2015, vol. 27, no. 3; *New Zealand Herald*, 9 November 1918.
3. In this chapter the names used are those that the men gave on enlistment. In this way their service records can be accessed from NZ Archives.
4. P. Cooke, J.H. Gray & K. Stead, *The Auckland Infantry* (Auckland: 3rd Battalion Regimental Association, 2010, 125).
5. 12/1539 William Alfred, ANZ AABK Series 18805, NZ Defence Force Personnel Files.
6. 'Among the wounded Maori soldiers', *Chronicles of the NZEF*, vol. 1, no. 2, 15 September 1916, 38.
7. 12/2078 Hono Paufai, ANZ AABK Series 18805, NZ Defence Force Personnel Files.
8. Cullen to Lenwood, 11 April 1917, LMS Records Niue 1910-1953, ATL Micro-MS-Coll-08-0701-1.
9. 3/1379 Make Allan, ANZ AABK Series 18805, NZ Defence Force Personnel Files. The author has worked with the family of Make Allan, Neki, and they have agreed to the inclusion here of medical details.
10. Christopher Pugsley, *Te Hokowhitu a Tu: The Maori Pioneer Battalion in the First World War* (Auckland: Reed Books, 1995, 55).
11. 13/2202 Jack Harrys, ANZ AABK Series 18805, NZ Defence Force Personnel Files.
12. Pugsley, *Te Hokowhitu a Tu*, 67.
13. Timothy Winegard, *Indigenous Peoples of the British Dominions and the First World War* (New York: Cambridge University Press, 2012, 185).

14. 20717 Mick Haller, ANZ AABK Series 18805, NZ Defence Force Personnel Files.
15. Pomare to Army Paymaster, 6 December 1916, ANZ AAYS 8638 AD1. Establishments and Recruitment-Fijian Contingent NZEF.
16. 38671 E.J. Cunningham and 40542 A.G. Godsmark, ANZ AABK Series 18805, NZ Defence Force Personnel Files.
17. Charles Head died in 1957 and lies in the RSA section of the Old Levin Cemetery. He appears on the Auckland cenotaph database.

10. THE AFTERMATH OF WAR

1. Imelda Bargas, 'The 1918 influenza pandemic': nzhistory.govt.nz. See also Geoffrey Rice, *Black November: The 1918 influenza pandemic in New Zealand* (Christchurch: Canterbury University Press, 2005).
2. Michael Field, *Mau: Samoa's struggle against New Zealand oppression* (Wellington: A.H. & A.W. Reed, 1984, ch. 3).
3. *AJHR* 1919, vol. 1 A–D, A-3, 18.
4. *AJHR* 1920, vol. 1 A–D, A-3, 14.
5. See *AJHR* 1919, vol. 1 A–D, A-3, 18, for evidence of this second contingent.
6. 'Pacific Islanders in the NZEF': nzhistory.govt.nz
7. *NZPD*, vol. 177, July–August 1916, 326.
8. Commander NZ Military Forces to Minister of Defence, 29 July 1918, re Pay of Gilbert Islanders attached to NZEF, ANZ AAYS 8638 714 9/188. Expeditionary Force Gilbert and Ellis Islands Contingent.
9. See Appendix 3 for the full lists.
10. Cornwall to Secretary for the Cook Islands, 6 June 1917, ANZ AAYS 8638 844 31/419/15. Finance and Accounts-Pay and allowances-Niue Islanders.
11. Cook Islands Dept to Resident Commissioner Niue, 28 June 1927, ANZ ACGA 8280 IT1. Niue-War medals, roll of honour, war graves.
12. Deryck Scarr, *Ratu Sukuna: Soldier, statesman, man of two worlds* (London: Macmillan Education, 1980, 54), quoting from Colonial Secretary's Office file 21/1752.
13. *Thames Star*, 25 August 1916. Vasau and Taleva are both buried in Hornchurch, England.
14. Talava Tuhipa-Turner, 'Honouring our warrior ancestors', quoted in Sean Mallon, Kolokesa Māhina-Tuai & Damon Salesa (eds), *Tangata o le Moana: New Zealand and the people of the Pacific* (Wellington: Te Papa Press, 2012, 158).
15. 'A welcome surprise. Mokoia's party at Niue', *Evening Post*, 4 March 1920.
16. 'Governor-general at Niue', *Auckland Star*, 31 May 1926.
17. J. Evison, Resident Commissioner, Niue, to Under Sec. Internal Affairs, Wellington, 18 July 1921, ANZ ACGO 8333 W2578 IA1. War Graves – Niue island. The men listed are Mitipauni, Ku, Pieti, Imiu, Aleke Nui, Uku, Muimatagi, Pulekanamata, Alotau and Leini.

18. Information from personnel records, ANZ AABK 18805.
19. Lowell Thomas, *The Sea Devil: The story of Count Felix von Luckner, the German war raider* (London: Heinemann, 1928, 263).
20. 'Lyttelton news', *Press*, 16 November 1918.
21. Village councillors included Uea, Mitihepi, Lagigie, Manetoa, Falaile, Tionetini, Tafua, Liuvaie, and Moana. Information supplied by Moira Enetama, Tāoga Niue, June 2017.
22. See Auckland Museum online cenotaph database for images of plaques for both men.
23. Application for naturalisation by [Te Fatumoana] Moana, Leon; Moana, Mrs Sarah, ANZ ACGO 8333 IA1.
24. Information on Godsmark gathered from email discussion with Aokuso Pavihi, 2017, and from shipping details and personal columns in newspapers. See paperspast online.
25. Information from the late Selwyn Wilson in an interview with the author, 2011.
26. Aokuso Pavihi, 'Anzac Days with my grandfather', unpublished manuscript, lent to author by Aokuso Pavihi, Patron of Niue RSA, 2017.
27. Information from *Tohi Tala Niue/Niue Newsletter*, PMB Doc 467 Reels 1–10.
28. Recollections of Private Maka. Personal papers held by Maka's son, the late Kalaisi Folau of Hakupu.
29. Private Tio. Interview taped in 1970s, Niue Museum.
30. J. Evison, Resident Commissioner, Niue, to Under Sec. Internal Affairs, Wellington, 18 July 1921, ANZ ACGO 8333 W2578 IA1. War Graves – Niue island.
31. Ibid. Resident Commissioner, Niue, to Secretary, Cook Islands Dept., 4 September 1929.
32. The author worked with the Niue government archivist Ligi Sisikefu in 1999 to locate and photograph all servicemen's burial sites on Niue. Only eight official headstones were found at the time. All photographs have been digitised and lodged with Tāoga Niue, Alofi.
33. John Pule, *Burn My Head in Heaven* (Auckland: Penguin Books, 1998, 55).
34. Memoirs of 16/1111 Private Puleoti as retold by his son Vahatau. Personal collection, Niue.

Bibliography

PUBLISHED WORKS

Baker, Paul, *King and Country Call: New Zealanders, conscription and the Great War*, Auckland: Auckland University Press, 1988.

Boyack, Nicholas & Jane Tolerton (eds), *In the Shadow of War: New Zealand soldiers talk about World War One and their lives*, Auckland: Penguin Books, 1990.

Chapman, Terry (ed.) *Niue: A history of the island*, Suva: Institute of Pacific Studies and Government of Niue, 1982.

Cody, J.F., *Man of Two Worlds: Sir Maui Pomare*, Wellington: A.H. & A.W. Reed, 1953.

Cooke, P., J.H. Gray & K. Stead, T*he Auckland Infantry*, Auckland: 3rd Battalion Regimental Association, 2010.

Cowan, James, *The Maoris in the Great War: A history of the New Zealand Native Contingent and the Pioneer Battalion. Official History of New Zealand's Effort in the Great War*, vol. III, Auckland: Whitcombe & Tombs, 1926.

Crawford, Peter, *Nomads of the Wind: A natural history of Polynesia*, London: BBC Books, 1993.

Drew, H.T.B. (ed), *The War Effort of New Zealand. Official History of New Zealand's Effort in the Great War*, vol. IV (Auckland: Whitcombe & Tombs, 1923).

Fenton, Damien, *New Zealand and the First World War: 1914–1919*, Auckland: Penguin Books, 2013.

Ferguson, Niall, *Empire: How Britain made the modern world*, London: Penguin Books, 2004.

Field, Michael, *Mau: Samoa's struggle against New Zealand oppression*, Wellington: A.H. & A.W. Reed, 1984.

Goiran, Hélène, 'Hero of Fiji as a soldier of France: Ratu Sukuna', in John Crawford, David Littlewood & James Watson (eds), *Experience of a Lifetime: People, personalities and leaders in the First World War*, Auckland: Massey University Press, 2016.

Hiery, H.J., *The Neglected War: The German South Pacific and the influence of World War I*, Honolulu: University of Hawai`i Press, 1995.

Jackson, Ashley, 'The Empire at war (1914–18)', *BBC History Magazine*, vol. 9, no. 11 (November 2008).

King, Michael, *Te Puea: A biography*, Auckland: Hodder & Stoughton, 1977.

Loeb, Edwin M., *History and Traditions of Niue*, Honolulu: Bishop Museum, 1926.

Lowell, Thomas, *The Sea Devil: The story of Count Felix von Luckner, the German war raider*, London: Heinemann, 1928.

Mackenzie, C.N. (ed.), *Chronicles of the NZEF*, London: New Zealand War Contingent Association, 1916–1919.

Māhina-Tuai, Kolokesa, 'FIA (Forgotten in Action): Pacific Islanders in the New Zealand Armed Forces', in Sean Mallon, Kolokesa Māhina-Tuai & Damon Salesa (eds), *Tangata o le Moana: New Zealand and the people of the Pacific*, Wellington: Te Papa Press, 2012.

Mallon, Sean, Kolokesa Māhina-Tuai & Damon Salesa (eds), *Tangata o le Moana: New Zealand and the people of the Pacific*, Wellington: Te Papa Press, 2012.

Mannox, Barbara, *Hornchurch and the New Zealand Connection*, London: Havering Library Service, 1993.

Muckle, Adrian, 'Kanak experiences of WWI: New Caledonia's tirailleurs and rebels', *History Compass*, vol. 6, no. 5, 2008, 1325–45.

O'Connor, P.S. 'The recruitment of Maori soldiers, 1914–1918', *Political Science*, no. 19, 1967.

Perfect, C.T., *Hornchurch During the Great War*, Colchester: Benham & Co., 1920.

Pointer, Margaret, *Tagi Tote e Loto Haaku – My Heart Is Crying a Little: Niue Island involvement in the Great War 1914–18*, trans. Kalaisi Folau, Suva: Institute of Pacific Studies and Government of Niue, 2000.

——, *Niue 1774–1974: 200 years of contact and change*, Dunedin: Otago University Press, 2015.

——, 'Niue: Bringing the history home', in Katie Pickles et al., *History Making a Difference: New approaches from Aotearoa*, Newcastle upon Tyne: Cambridge Scholars Publishing, 2017.

Pugsley, Christopher, *Te Hokowhitu a Tu: The Maori Pioneer Battalion in the First World War*, Auckland: Reed, 1995.

Pule, John, *Burn My Head in Heaven*, Auckland: Penguin Books, 1998.

Salesa, Damon, 'New Zealand's Pacific', in Giselle Byrne (ed.), *The New Oxford History of New Zealand*, Melbourne: Oxford University Press Australia & New Zealand, 2009.

Scarr, Deryck, *Ratu Sukuna: Soldier, statesman, man of two worlds*, London: Macmillan Education, 1980.

Scott, Dick, *Would a Good Man Die? Niue Island, New Zealand and the late Mr Larsen*, Auckland: Southern Cross Books & Hodder & Stoughton, 1993.

Sherwood, Marika, 'Racism by omission', *BBC History Magazine*, 29 December 2009: www.historyextra.com/contributions

Smith, S. Percy, *Niue: The island and its people*, Suva: Institute of Pacific Studies, 1983.

Soutar, Monty, *Whitiki: Māori in the First World War*, Auckland: David Bateman, 2018.

Sperlich, Wolfgang (ed.), *Tohi Vagahau Niue/Niue Language Dictionary*, Honolulu: Government of Niue and University of Hawai`i, 1997.

Stewart, H., *France. Official History of New Zealand's Effort in the Great War*, vol. II, Auckland: Whitcombe & Tombs, 1921.

Thomas, Nicholas, *Islanders: The Pacific in the Age of Empire*, New Haven & London: Yale University Press, 2010.

Truttman, Lisa, 'To serve and die so far away from home', *NZ Legacy*, vol. 27, no. 3, 2015.

Weddell, Howard, *Soldiers from the Pacific: The story of Pacific Islanders in the New Zealand Expeditionary Force in World War I*, Defence of New Zealand Study Group, 2015.

Winegard, Timothy, *Indigenous Peoples of the British Dominions and the First World War*, New York: Cambridge University Press, 2012.

UNPUBLISHED

Alexander Turnbull Library, National Library of New Zealand, Wellington

Gordon, Colin M., 'Life of a hospital orderly', MS Papers 2514

Gray, Randolph Norman, Papers relating to World War One, MS-Group-2302

LMS Records relating to Niue Island 1861–1910, Micro-MS-0471

LMS Records Niue 1910–1953, Micro-MS-Coll-08-0701 (PMB 701)

Tohi Tala Niue, Niue newsletter, Alofi: Office of Resident Commissioner, 1953–1980, PMB 467

Archives New Zealand, Wellington

AABK New Zealand Defence Force, Personnel Files

AAYS Army Department

ACGA Island Territories Department

ACGO Department of Internal Affairs

ACID War Archives

ADBQ Hon. Sir James Allen

Auckland War Memorial Museum

Fitchett, Wilfred, 'The diaries of a front line soldier', Auckland War Memorial Museum Library

NSW State Library, Australia

Clarke, Eric Roy, war diaries, 17 Nov. 1915–14 Dec. 1916. Reference Code 862206

ONLINE

http://paperspast.natlib.govt.nz New Zealand newspapers online

http://trove.nla.gov.au Australian newspapers online

www.nzhistory.govt.nz/war/pacific-islanders-nzef

www.nzhistory.govt.nz/war/pacific-aftermath

www.nzhistory.govt.nz/war/anzac-day-pacific

www.nzhistory.govt.nz/media/video/falaoa-and-niueans-great-war-story – a video that tells the story of Falaoa and Mrs Lawes

www.nzhistory.govt.nz/handsonhistory/downloads-and-podcasts – 'I am the island of Niue, a small child that stands up to help' – podcast August 2014 by Margaret Pointer

www.radionz.co.nz/national/programmes/sunday/audio/201760214/indigenous-and-pacific-experiences-in-the-first-world-war – Monty Soutar, Damon Salesa & Gary Oakley discuss the involvement of Māori, Pacific and Aboriginal troops in World War I

www.aucklandmuseum.com/war-memorial/online-cenotaph – database of all men and women who have served in New Zealand Forces in all wars

www.bl.uk/world-war-one/articles/colonial-troops – Santanu Das, 'Experiences of colonial troops', January 2014

OFFICIAL PUBLICATIONS

AJHR – Appendices to the Journal of the House of Representatives
NZPD – New Zealand Parliamentary Debates

A NOTE ON USING RESOURCES

For those wishing to access individual personnel files of Niuean men who served in the NZEF, Archives New Zealand provides an online service and all World War I files have now been digitised.

Go to the official Archives New Zealand site. Use the Archway search engine. Under 'simple search', type in the name of your family member and click. Follow the prompts through to the actual copies of all documents in that man's file. Note: some genealogy websites offer access to this site but require you to pay. The official Archives New Zealand site is free to use.

An alternative, and in some cases more successful way of searching for a record is to write in the serviceman's regimental number. That will bring up the file with possibly a different spelling of the name.

Readers may also find the Auckland Museum He Toa Taumata Rau Online Cenotaph database useful: www.aucklandmuseum.com/war-memorial/online-cenotaph. This is an ongoing project to record the names and details of all personnel who have served in the New Zealand Forces from the 19th century through to the present day.

Most of the Niue men are already listed in the Online Cenotaph database, as all names have been transcribed there from Margaret Pointer, *Tagi Tote e Loto Haaku*. Families are able to add further information and images, and some have now added headstone photos of Niuean men.

If you wish to contribute to the site, follow the prompts. Material must be authenticated before it can be uploaded to the site.

Index

Page numbers in **bold** refer to illustrations.